How to Negotiate

Persuade using the power of influence and conversation skills to increase your confidence in negotiation.

Natasha Baker & James Fisher

Copyright © Baker Publishing

All rights reserved.

No part of this publication may be reproduced, distributed, or transmitted in any form or by any means, including photocopying, recording, or other electronic or mechanical methods, without the prior written permission of the publisher, except in the case of brief quotations embodied in critical reviews and certain other non-commercial uses permitted by copyright law.

Table of Contents

How to Negotiate Persuade using the power of influence and conversation skills to increase your confidence in negotiation.

Natasha Baker & James Fisher

- Chapter One: We Can All Be Negotiators
- Negotiation is Everywhere!
- Negotiation in a Professional Setting
- Negotiations at Home
- What Is Negotiation?
- Do You Feel Too Scared to Negotiate?
- Good Negotiators Are Made, Not Born
- Traits of a Good Negotiator
- Chapter Two: Easily Setting the Scene for Negotiation
- Negotiations Gone Wrong
- Dealing With Job Offers
- Getting Ready for Negotiation
- How To Actually Prepare
- The 80/20 Rule
- Beware the Common Negotiation Missteps
- Chapter Three: Best Practices in Negotiation
- Defining Givers, Takers and Matchers
- Give and Take – A Revolutionary Approach to Success
- Best Practices to Follow in a Negotiation
- Making Counter Offers
- How To Not Show Neediness
- Controlling Emotions such as Anger and Anxiety
- Chapter Four: Negotiation For ALL

Negotiation Fail #1

Negotiation Fail #2

Negotiation Fail #3

Negotiation Fail #4

Finding the Confidence to Negotiate

Number One Tip: Negotiate for Others

Chapter Five: Introducing the Six KEY Principles of Persuasion

Persuading People to Say Yes

How to Trigger Reciprocity

Using Reciprocity in a Job Interview or Promotion Scenario

The Principle of Scarcity

How to Use the Scarcity Principle in a Workplace Situation

Using the Authority Principle in Job Interviews and Negotiations

Using the Liking Principle in Job Interviews and Similar Situations

Chapter Six: Effective Negotiation in Professional or Serious Settings

Establishing Trust and Likability

Building the Trust

How to Negotiate with Someone You Don't Trust

What to Do when Negotiation Fails

Chapter Seven: Negotiating in your Personal Life

Relationship Negotiation!

A Quick Word about Negotiating with Friends

The Abilene Paradox

Negotiating with Children

Chapter Eight: Effective Body Language in Negotiation

How to Develop Rapport

Communication Cues to Match

How to Read Other People's Body Language

How to Detect Deception

Chapter Nine: Persuasive Language: Getting People to Yes in Negotiation

The Most Powerful Words in the English Language

Chapter One: We Can All Be Negotiators

"Let us never negotiate out of fear. But let us never fear to negotiate."
John F. Kennedy

I'll let you into a little secret… don't tell anyone who didn't know me in my formative years, but I was a painfully shy child. An awkward teenager too. I used to struggle to speak to anyone I didn't know, and God help me if there was a boy I liked… I couldn't even look in his direction without blushing beetroot red. Not the best way to get noticed.

Fast forward a decade or two later (a lady never reveals her age), and there I was, running one of the biggest news websites in the world, negotiating with people for a living and managing a team of 50-plus men and women.

I dealt with hiring and firing, employment contracts and settlements as well as pay rises, my own and others. I negotiated exclusive deals for photographs, content, freelancers and more. I oversaw budgets and fought almost to the death with bean counters who wanted to slash costs every five minutes or so. Because of course you can run a 24/7 online news operation with one person and a typewriter.

It's fair to say that I've probably forgotten just as many important negotiations as I remember.

On a personal note, I once negotiated an overnight pay rise of £15,000 per annum for myself in my current job – and then I did it again a few years later. Yes, I'm proud of that to this day.

Why am I telling you this?

I promise I'm not just tooting my horn for the sake of it, and of course, nothing is ever just about the money, as welcome as it was at the time. I'm trying to make a point, a demonstration: You see, if I can learn the art of negotiation, anyone can. I'd like to think that terribly shy girl grew up to be a strong, capable woman, but I am still no more attuned to the subtleties and strategies of negotiation than anyone else. I had to learn this stuff too, often on the job, just like you.

I don't claim to be the foremost expert on the subject; I'm still just an ordinary person who had the good luck to have had some extraordinary opportunities. Ones that gave me plenty of scope to learn all about the power of negotiation and persuasion, and to put into practice my new skills time and time again.

Did I get everything right the first time? Of course not. But I learned from my mistakes, adapted my strategies and honed my skills. And now I want to share them with you.
Do you know what amazes me to this day? How universal negotiation skills are. Once you learn the basics and understand the strategies, you can use your improved negotiation abilities in all sorts of situations.

I'd like to think I'm just as effective haggling over the price of a t-shirt in the market as I am negotiating my employment contract, for instance. Or negotiating service contracts. And trust me, I need all my persuasion skills at hand for the day-to-day of dealing with my twin daughters. Nothing can humble you quite as effectively as raising a pre-schooler, let alone two!

Negotiation is Everywhere!

Here's why learning and improving upon your persuasion skills is important… because life is nothing but negotiation. It's true. Whether you recognize it or not, you're negotiating all day every day, especially if you have children, but even if you don't.

From the moment you plead/ cajole/ threaten/ beg or cry for your three-year-old not to get out of bed at 6am, to the minute you offer them 'One-Last-Cuddle, OK!' so they'll go to sleep, it never stops.

And what do you do after that? Promptly negotiate with your other half what to watch on TV, decide who cooks the dinner, choose between red wine or white (white, always white), or, for you lucky free and single folks, maybe plan where to go that evening. Or, if you're conscientious, you might sit down and work out your plan of action for the next day at work and how you'll achieve the things you want... that may well be preparation for a negotiation as well.

At home, at work, at a friend's, in the store, when out and about... negotiation can be major or mundane, but we can't escape it.

As the authors Roger Fisher and William Ury, of the seminal book, **'Getting to Yes: Negotiating Agreement Without Giving In'** say, *"Like it or not, you are a negotiator. Negotiation is a fact of life... Everyone negotiates something every day"*.

Negotiation in a Professional Setting

You're more likely to recognize instances of negotiation or persuasion in a work or professional setting, than at home. (At home it can slip by unnoticed, couched in comfortable relationships).

At work, in contrast, negotiation is often more formal. We negotiate hiring, firing, performance, deadlines, scope, deliverables, fees, partnerships, agreements, even lunch! You might need to negotiate with your subordinates about unexpected overtime, your boss about a new work assignment, the bank about a business loan, suppliers over inventory and more. Some of your most difficult negotiations may come about when trying to handle conflicts with co-workers.

I'm not exaggerating when I say that negotiation is your MOST effective tool of influence inside a company and is more important than ever in today's world.

Very few of us have jobs for life anymore, so we need to know how to negotiate to keep up with the changing nature of business. We will need to renegotiate our positions throughout our careers, ready to adapt to new opportunities (or curveballs) that come our way.

Businesses nowadays are operating in uncertain but exciting times. For instance, the pace of technology alone has transformed industry in ways that were unthinkable just a few years ago. Companies can now make more for less, grow at a faster pace, use the latest technologies and IT, interconnect using the Internet of Things, and use software and data accumulation to ensure practically flawless production.
If you specialize in one of those industries, negotiation is your most effective tool for keeping yourself relevant. Asking for the training you need, convincing bosses to take a chance on you, knowing how to operate in an ambiguous environment… it's the key to being at the top of your game. To being at the forefront of the advances and not left behind by them.

The innovations of recent years and the 24/7 world they are driving have made the world move faster and seem smaller at the same time. The impact of globalization, for instance, adds another dimension to negotiation. Now we must learn to negotiate with suppliers, clients and colleagues from cultural backgrounds different to our own.

As Leigh Thompson, author of **'The Mind and Heart of the Negotiator'**, says, negotiation is an *"interpersonal decision-making process" that is "necessary whenever we cannot achieve our objectives single-handedly."* The above would certainly qualify.

The negotiations you face may not always be on par with the hurdles facing the U.S./North Korea nuclear talks or Brexit negotiators, for instance, (now there is a job I don't envy: I imagine they really need that white wine at the end of an evening), but they can significantly affect a business's bottom line. And therefore, your future.

Have I convinced you of the importance of negotiation yet?

Negotiations at Home

As I've already touched upon, the discussions don't stop at home either, do they? Perhaps you and your other half disagree on certain aspects of child-rearing and need to negotiate your way through it. This is certainly true for my marriage; my husband comes from a very different background (country, culture and religion!) to me, and there is a lot that we'd naturally do differently to each other. He's much more laid back than I am; often it works because he calms me down, but at other times, we negotiate our way forward carefully.

You might need to decide who walks the dog, for instance, or discuss something that can't be solved via Rock, Paper, Scissors. The big topics – how much you're saving, if your aged parents can live with you, how best to secure your own or your children's financial future, whether to move home, which home to buy (lots of negotiation once you decide as well) etc…

And if you want a real challenge, try to negotiate with a toddler to eat his or her peas!

What Is Negotiation?

One of the simplest descriptions of negotiation I've ever read goes back to *Getting to Yes*. It may be more than 30 years since it was first published, but it still has a lot to teach us. The authors describe negotiation as *a "back-and-forth communication designed to reach an agreement when you and the other side have some interests that are shared and others that are opposed."*

Other experts define negotiation similarly. In their book 'Judgment in Managerial Decision Making', Max H. Bazerman and Don A. Moore say, *"When two or more parties need to reach a joint decision but have different preferences, they negotiate."*
Here's the problem though… not only do we not even realize that we're negotiating at times, we're often just not very good at it.

The idea of negotiation – asking for a salary increase, discussing the state of our marriage, negotiating a merger – can turn many of us into anxiety-ridden shadows of our former selves. We fear to be too assertive, not assertive enough, too confrontational, insensitive, or too weak. Sometimes all at the same time!

Do You Feel Too Scared to Negotiate?

Negotiating a pay rise with an existing employer or asking for a higher salary after a new job offer are common areas of reluctance for many of us. We are leaving money on the table because we just don't feel comfortable negotiating for more.

According to U.S. staffing firm Robert Half, only 39% of workers even tried to negotiate salary with their last job offer. Of those questioned, more men than women (45% to 34%) said they negotiated for pay. Reports also show that more than 60% of millennial women, for instance, don't know how to ask for a pay rise.

Women's reluctance to ask for what they are worth is a particular problem, say many experts.
Carol Sankar, founder of The Confidence Factor for Women, told Forbes that the act of negotiating is viewed very differently by the sexes. *"For women, negotiation is seen as an improper act of appearing 'greedy' or 'desperate.'"* Men, meanwhile, are *"encouraged to ask, renegotiate compensation agreements, partnerships and more."*

I'll be talking about the real and perceived differences between men and women's negotiating styles later in this book and offering advice. Note that nothing above says that women are not as effective as men at negotiating, just that they are more reluctant.

The reluctance isn't just limited to gender either. A 2016 survey from Glassdoor also revealed that older workers are negotiating less than their younger counterparts, potentially contributing to a U.S. gender pay gap that increases with age. Glassdoor's Economic Research reveals that the adjusted pay gap for 18-24-year-olds is

2.2%, compared to an overall average gap of 5.4% and 10.5% for workers over 55.

For many of us, negotiating for salary just isn't something we're comfortable with. Here's the irony: according to Salary.com, 84% of employers expect potential new employees to negotiate money during the interview stage. Indeed, according to CareerBuilder, two-thirds of those people who are brave enough to ask for a raise actually get one.

There's a lesson for all of us there!

Good Negotiators Are Made, Not Born

I'll be examining the reasons a lot of us are so reticent to negotiate throughout this book and offering solutions to the common fears – rejection, fear of losing your job, a dislike of negotiation itself and worrying that you're not worth the money. Quick point: I bet you are!

Rest assured, however, that if you're reticent when it comes to negotiation, you are not alone.

The good news is that good negotiators can be made and are not always born.

"Very few of us would describe ourselves as 'negotiation naturals'," says Prof. Joan Roure of IESE Business School's Department of Entrepreneurship and Negotiation Teaching Unit in Barcelona. *"Fortunately, it's a skill that can be developed which starts by gaining a deeper awareness of our unique style and the distinct phases of the negotiating process."*

It's important to believe you can negotiate too.

In a University of California study, professor Laura Kray of the Berkeley Haas School of Business proved how such a belief in the ability to learn negotiation skills improved results for the better.

During the study, certain participants were told negotiation traits were largely inherited, while others were told negotiation skills could be learned. Those told the latter performed significantly better than those who believed such skills were only inheritable.

The takeaway? Believe you can learn to be a better negotiator and you're already a step closer to being one.

Traits of a Good Negotiator

There are various traits that can make a good negotiator. Some may be innate personality traits, but others can be learned or improved upon.

Some are obvious – common sense, communication ability, ability to stay calm under pressure… all good skills to have in most situations. But others are harder to pinpoint or add a depth to our negotiations that would otherwise be missing.

Emotional intelligence is the ability to understand others and empathize, to appreciate why they feel and react the way they do. The ability to 'read' your clients, suppliers, potential employer, co-workers, family members is one of the most effective negotiation skills you can have. And unlike IQ (traditional intelligence), EQ or Emotional Intelligence can be learned.
I would add a few others to the list as well – strong self-esteem (confidence in yourself is a pre-requisite before even beginning the negotiation), personal integrity (the best negotiators don't sell each other down the river) and planning skills are all important.

It's crucial that you never enter a negotiation without being fully briefed and without doing your homework. You'll need to understand market conditions, have product knowledge and much, much more to give yourself a good chance of negotiating what you need. You'll find a more comprehensive look at staging a negotiation and the sort of things that are imperative to research in my next chapter.

These traits form the basis of potentially good negotiation, but you must learn how to use them, of course. This book will show you how. In some cases, you may be able to compensate for weakness in one area by strengthening another.

Once you appreciate that you can learn and improve on your negotiation skills – and picking up this book is an excellent first step towards that goal – you just need to find the opportunity to use what you've learned.

Luckily for us, as we now know, life offers plentiful situations to practice our negotiation skills.

As Princess Leia, sorry, Carrie Fisher once said, "Everything is negotiable. Whether or not the negotiation is easy is another thing."

Luckily for you, this book is chock-full of tips and advice destined to make your next negotiations easier and more fruitful… whether it's finally asking the boss for a raise, agreeing business unit requirements, selling your new product to the market, or even negotiating the chores with your teenager.

You'll need all the help you can get for the last one, so carry on reading!

Chapter Two: Easily Setting the Scene for Negotiation

"Diplomacy is the art of letting someone else have your way."
Sir David Frost

Have you ever walked into a room and been completely blind-sided by a meeting that was nothing like you imagined? I have and let me tell you, it's no fun.

In my case, it was a routine update that turned into an unannounced budget meeting, complete with negotiations over costs, people and jobs. The surprise agenda was deliberate, of course; an attempt to knock me off my game so that certain unappreciative parties could hack our budget to pieces. (If you're already starting to suspect this may be a recurring theme, you'd be correct. Unfortunately).

Thankfully, I managed to stand my ground, but at the end of the meeting, I felt mentally and physically exhausted. And betrayed. I'd shared an after-work drink with the two instigators just the week before with the aim of maintaining good relations. Ironic, hey?

No matter how professional you like to think you are, you're going to face situations that evoke strong emotion. We're all just human, after all. Anger, shock, betrayal, frustration, disappointment… a bad negotiation can stir up all of the above. Of course, emotions have no place in such meetings, so you'll need to learn to swallow them down and stay objective. Keep your eye on the prize, so to speak.

One of the best ways to avoid feeling angry or frustrated in a negotiation is to be prepared. If I'd asked around the company ahead of my meeting, for instance, I would have learned that cost-cutting was on the agenda, and I wasn't the first person to be 'surprised' in such a manner. Yes, it was a low-down thing to do, but had I known what to expect, I could have prepared for it and played them at their own game. (In case you're wondering, not all negotiations need to be so adversarial. This one was deliberately so; certain high-up factions of my company thrived on Machiavellian behavior. It didn't do much for my blood pressure – one reason why I'm no longer working there – but it certainly honed my negotiation skills.)

Negotiations can often be tough, but they're harder still if you don't have the information you need. Many people mistakenly think they need to concentrate only on what they themselves want to get out of the meeting, but the truth is that knowing the other person's agenda can make or break your own.

Doing your homework doesn't stop once you leave school, as much as you might wish it did, and knowing how to set the stage for an effective negotiation is an important skill to master. Without it, you're going to struggle to get what you want.

Negotiations Gone Wrong

Let me guess… one of the reasons you picked up this book in the first place is that your recent negotiations haven't gone as well as they could.

Perhaps you too were blindsided by the other party's behavior for whatever reason. Maybe they rejected your price suggestion outright or refused to negotiate on an issue that you wrongly assumed they would discuss. Perhaps you failed to appreciate the financial pressure they were under from outside elements and it trickled over into your negotiations.

Alternatively, maybe you're frustrated that you didn't sell yourself as well as you could have at a recent interview or asked for the money you deserved. You balked at asking for a higher salary and now you can't stop thinking about the money you left on the table. You accepted their 'final offer' but you've since suspected it was only an opening gambit.

You may have even been able to thrash out a deal/ compromise, but it took a lot of threats and conflict to get there. Now you're worried your relationship is irreparably damaged as a result, and you're starting to wonder if negotiations must always be so confrontational. Tip: they don't.

"If you are planning on doing business with someone again, don't be too tough in the negotiations. If you're going to skin a cat, don't keep it as a house cat."
Marvin Levin

I'm willing to bet that a lot of these 'failures' or 'could do betters' on your negotiation report card stem from one thing: a lack of homework. You simply weren't prepared for what faced you.

You hadn't realized your biggest supplier was having financial issues due to an overseas contractor pulling their business, for instance. So, you were unprepared when they tried to renegotiate your agreement. Or you walked into a salary negotiation with a figure in mind, only to belatedly discover that you'd sold yourself short compared to the rest of the market.

There are always things we can do better; the minute we decide we know it all is the minute we start to slip backward, too arrogant to learn. As Anthony J. D'Angelo said, *"Develop a passion for learning. If you do, you will never cease to grow."*

"If you come to a negotiation table saying you have the final truth, that you know nothing but the truth and that is final, you will get nothing."
Harri Holkeri

In short, poor preparation has scuppered many, many negotiations, and can come from either side. Take the real-life example below...

Dealing With Job Offers

Rebecca, a chief sub-editor for a large regional UK newspaper group, was over the moon to be approached by a head-hunter offering a potential job in the U.S, launching the UK version of a popular U.S. website. She expressed her interest, interviews soon followed, one in London and another in New York; both sides agreed she was the perfect person for the job… and salary negotiations began.

Rebecca knew she wasn't asking for much. She'd reached the end of the line in her current job and had always wanted to live in New York. *"I know I probably should have played hardball, but I just couldn't bring myself to,"* says Rebecca. *"I asked for three weeks' vacation as opposed to the two they offered, but otherwise as long as I got a comparable salary to my current job, I was happy to accept."*

Rebecca knew her potential bosses were excited by her hire; it seemed a done deal aside from the salary and contract negotiations. *"They were talking about sending contracts out as soon as the HR manager and I agreed a salary. It seemed a formality."*

And then the offer finally came… for £20,000 less than Rebecca was already earning.

"I was devastated and to be honest, offended. I really thought they valued and respected me, and then they made a crazy offer that I couldn't possibly accept. All that time we'd spent negotiating was wasted and I couldn't understand the difference in attitude".
As much as she knew it wasn't feasible, Rebecca even priced up studio apartments in New York to see if she could make the 'new salary' work. She couldn't.

Rebecca shakes her head. *"There was no way I could afford anything in any of the decent areas of New York and I refused to consider sharing a house or an apartment. I'd lived on my own for years now, and it felt like such a backward move to have housemates again, especially because my new bosses just didn't think I was worth a decent wage."*

Sadly, she declined the job and assumed that would be the end of it.

It wasn't. *"Unbelievably the HR woman came back to me the next day and said there'd been a terrible mistake. I assumed she might offer me a little bit more money, but I'd already resolved not to take it unless the offer matched my current salary. It turns out that it did!"*

The terrible mistake? The HR woman hadn't done her homework properly and had failed to translate dollars into pounds adequately. She offered £20,000 less than she had been instructed to (after some dubious dollars to pounds computations) and had been raked over the coals for it.

Luckily, the error was spotted and corrected, and Rebecca could accept the job!

Both Rebecca and the HR woman who nearly lost her job over the mistake now appreciate the importance of being prepared and doing your research.

Don't underestimate how much preparedness and pre-knowledge contribute to successful negotiation. If you're not already a top-notch negotiator, do not even try to fly by the seat of your pants. (And to be fair, no top-notch negotiator worth his or her salt becomes that way by failing to do their research).

Not doing your homework sinks deals, so let's look at how you can set the scene for a positive civil negotiation – one in which both parties treat each other respectfully and manage to come to a mutually agreeable decision. Yes, it can happen!

Getting Ready for Negotiation

First things first: let's talk about a few things that have no place in negotiation: anger, luck, threats and emotion. What should play a part in effective negotiations? Doing your homework, discipline and having the courage to go after what you want.

I'm going to talk in detail about the best practices of negotiation in our next chapter, but before we even go there, it's important to set the stage from the get-go. If you don't frame the negotiation in a positive way, you're going to start on the back foot/ shoot yourself in the foot/ suffer the agony of defeat. Pick your pun. (Sorry, couldn't resist. I don't have a feet fetish, I promise.)

The following tenets to live by when negotiating will prevent any extremity-related issues.

How To Actually Prepare

"By failing to prepare, you are preparing to fail."
Benjamin Franklin

Benjamin Franklin knew what he was talking about: walk into a negotiation without preparation, and you're sinking your efforts from the start. Research the party you're negotiating with if you don't already know them (and even if you do!) to identify their strengths and weaknesses. Ideally, talk to business associates of the other party to get a feel for his or her negotiating style. You may be able to use this to your advantage.

You shouldn't walk into a salary negotiation without knowing what you are worth – and ideally knowing what others in similar roles in your industry are paid – so that you can negotiate with facts on your side. Otherwise, your boss or potential boss could tell you that you're already overpaid compared to others doing the same job elsewhere (or try to pay you less than others), and you won't know enough to dispute it.

Similarly, if you're a buyer, the best way to tell if someone is trying to bluff you is by being thoroughly familiar with the product or service that you are negotiating for. If you are unprepared for the negotiations, the other side will no doubt recognize it and potentially take advantage.

You wouldn't try to buy antiques without knowing a fair amount about, well, historical old things, would you? Particularly what makes them unique and valuable. The more research you can do, the better.

Get any lowdown that you can about the other party's agenda; we all have one. Knowing what they hope to achieve can help you prepare for the meeting adequately. If you're happy to agree to provide what they want, make sure you're getting what you want too. If you're not happy with their aims, here's your chance to get ahead of the negotiation.

Oh, and one final point – when you do know all the above and more, try to be objective about it. Using the information at your fingertips works best if you're calm and detached about it, making it a central plank in your argument and not just a complaint of a personal nature. Of course, you may still want a subjective win, but approach it with an objective outlook and it's much more likely.

Know Your Goal
Most negotiators have a goal or price target in mind before negotiations even start. Ideally, it will be realistic given the potential constraints each side faces. These could include pressure to meet sales goals, a direction from above, budget limitations and more.

Of course, the goal may change depending on alterations in scope during the meeting, and the original goal shouldn't necessarily restrict your offer or counteroffer.

The point is, however, that you shouldn't go into negotiation with no other goal than negotiating. You are there to settle on something. Know your target. It will give a purposeful direction to the negotiations.

Have a Plan

Forget being a man with a van, you want to be the man (or woman) with a plan. Knowing your goal isn't enough… you want to have a plan, hypothetical scenarios and contingencies, to get you there.

Prepare for all the potential obstacles you can imagine before you walk into the room and know what your reaction should be beforehand. It might make it easier to deal with unforeseen obstacles as well. What if the negotiator insists that the price is set? Will, you walk away, or decide to meet it? Come up with another offer?

Planning helps do away with some of the surprises and help you avoid impulsive reactions. Of course, you can't prepare for everything, but it helps to have a general idea of how you would react in certain circumstances.

Make sure you know your BATNA too, as it's described in *Getting to Yes*. That's your Best Alternative to a Negotiated Agreement, i.e., what will you do if the deal doesn't pan out? If you walk away from the table, what are your other alternatives? Make sure you have your backup plans.

Exude Confidence
Setting the stage for a successful negotiation starts from the first moment you walk through the door. (Well, to be fair, it starts well ahead of that when you do your homework, but first impressions begin the second you meet the other party). Confidence, looking strong and self-assured, will instantly give you more negotiating power.

Lacking the confidence? Don't let the other side know that; as the saying goes, fake it until you make it.

I'm dedicating a whole chapter later in the book to body language and you can bet there's a section in there on the best body language to use on your side of the table. For now, though, quick cribbing, make sure you walk tall, shake hands firmly, shoulders back, make eye contact while talking, speak articulately and avoid fidgeting.

Practice

Wondering how you can 'fake it until you make it'? Practice, practice, practice. The more negotiations you experience, the better you're going to get – practice really does help, after all. But you can practice the small stuff before you walk into your next negotiation as well. All you need is a mirror and a few prepared responses.

If you're going for a job interview, for instance, practice a couple of prepared responses or a justification for why you deserve the job/ deserve the pay you're asking for in front of the mirror. When you do it for real, you'll seem more natural and less awkward. Just be sure not to over-practice: you don't want the answers to seem glib, too rehearsed or robotic.

<u>Establish your Leverage</u>
As well as discovering the other party's weaknesses, be sure to take advantage of your strengths as well. Identify your leverage. Perhaps you're the only supplier of a particular product or your product is in great demand; both give you tremendous leverage and bargaining power when it comes to naming your price.

Establish your leverage early in the negotiation to ensure you don't have to play catch-up.

The 80/20 Rule

Here's a neat little tip – decide up-front what sort of negotiator you want to be. A Harvard study years ago revealed that 80% of people adopt the same strategy in a negotiation – namely, to size up the other person's negotiating stance and take it from there. So, if the other negotiator wants to collaborate, they will collaborate, Or, if they play hardball, the negotiator will respond in kind.

It sounds sensible in a way, doesn't it? But then consider the other 20% of negotiators not mentioned above.

Who are these people? They are the negotiators who choose to be more assertive and who desire to set the tone, rather than follow it.

The good news? Most often, the other party follows their lead no matter what stage they set because they are likely dealing with one of the 80%, with someone who is waiting for the other party to set the tone.

So, right here, right now, decide that you want to be one of the proactive 20%, and lead the negotiations from the start. You will significantly improve your chances of success by doing so.

Beware the Common Negotiation Missteps

Doing the above as a matter of course should help to set the negotiation for a productive meeting, but it's just as important that you avoid some of the common mistakes or pitfalls of inexperienced negotiators.

As Eldonna Lewis-Fernandez, author of **Think Like a Negotiator**, says: *"You have to go out and learn to negotiate–it's not a natural skill. It's like playing baseball; you have to do it to get good at it."*

She points out that there is no switch to make you an immediate expert; instead, you must take the time to learn the art of negotiation and work through the fear you probably feel at the beginning.

According to Lewis-Fernandez, the five most common mistakes made during negotiations include:

<u>1. Lack of Confidence</u>

"The trick to negotiation was to hold all the cards going in and, even if you didn't, to try to look as though you did."
Eoin Colfer, Artemis Fowl

As I mentioned in my last chapter, many people, often women, believe that negotiation is 'greedy or desperate' or is only effective when done by someone with experience and/ or a brazen personality.

As such, many people shy away from negotiations assuming they can't possibly be good at it when really all that is needed is preparation and tenacity.

Projecting an aura of confidence which I will cover in my chapter on body language, especially one with a 'heart', can be endearing, says Lewis-Fernandez, giving the 'opposition a less defensive stance'.

My father is one of the best negotiators I know, mostly for his amazing tenacity. Every six months like clockwork, he would march into the boss's office and demand a pay rise, no embarrassment or hesitation. His philosophy was 'if you don't ask, you don't get'.

I can imagine the boss cringing every time he saw him, knowing it was that time again. My father, a bluff straight-talking Northerner, obviously asked with charm and objectivity, as he continued to work for him for more than two decades.

And he did often receive a pay rise!

The key was my father's confidence and objectivity: he didn't get offended if turned down for a pay-rise, just warned the boss he would be back again in six months. It wasn't personal, just business. It's hard to take offense at that.

2. Failing to remember that (almost) everything is negotiable

Never assume something is non-negotiable. Rules are made to be broken, and powerful negotiators can propose viable alternatives that allow opponents to negotiate 'off-limit' topics, says Lewis-Fernandez. Herb Cohen, author of You Can Negotiate Anything and Negotiate This, agrees that 'virtually everything is negotiable', assuming it's the 'product of a negotiation'.

However, Cohen, who has advised presidents in hostage negotiations, points out that moral, ethical and religious principles are the exception. They are not flexible or negotiable. The 10 Commandments, for instance, are both literally and figuratively written in stone (and stored in the Ark of the Covenant, according to the Bible).

Everything else, however, is fair game.

3. Failing to Build Relationships before Negotiating
Negotiating with strangers is a difficult nut to crack…building relationships first can transform a negotiation into a civil and effective meeting of minds. How better to know what motivates, frustrates and is important to a person than to have a genuine conversation with them first?

Managing relationships during negotiations are particularly important when future business and your reputation could rely on it.

As Dale Carnegie, of **How to Win Friends and Influence People** fame, says: *"You can close more business in two months by becoming interested in other people than you can in two years by trying to get people interested in you."*

Carnegie knows what he's talking about. How to Win Friends and Influence People was listed number 19 on Time Magazine's 100 most influential books.

4. Being too scared to ask for what you want
It sounds contradictory, doesn't it, but you'd be surprised how many people struggle in negotiations because they're too scared to ask for what they want. It could be fear of rejection or not wanting to look greedy, but how can you achieve your goals if you won't state them out loud?

Rejection will happen; there's no avoiding it, but the best way to deal with it is to realize that it's never personal. Be as thick-skinned as my father above, and you'll handle it like a pro.

Here's something else useful to know too – according to numerous studies, on average people say no to a sale FIVE TIMES before they say yes. So, a no isn't necessarily their final answer; it just means that you haven't sufficiently proved why you deserve whatever you're asking for. So, try again. Consider it a challenge.

5. Be a Chatterbox

Lewis-Fernandez's final mistake warns that it is possible to talk too much and to turn people off a purchase or away from an agreement. Effective negotiators need to be comfortable with the power of silence; it can be your most powerful weapon.

As essayist and award-winning Times magazine writer Lance Morrow sums it up: *"Never forget the power of silence, that massively disconcerting pause which goes on and on and may at last induce an opponent to babble and backtrack nervously."*

You've probably gathered by now that there's a lot of skill involved in a negotiation, both in setting the stage for an effective productive meeting and in holding the face-to-face discussions themselves.

I'm going to share my tips for the latter in my next chapter.

I'll talk about the power of listening, reveal some of the demons that ruin negotiation (and how to avoid them), and discuss psychologist and influential author Adam Grant's fundamental rules of negotiation. I'll also look at the gender issue in negotiation, examining in more detail why women are less likely to negotiate than men. That's in chapter three. You'll want to read that; it has some vitally important information for anyone wanting to hone their negotiation skills.

You'll also want to carry on reading to chapter four too, where I reveal the Six Principles of Persuasion, as detailed by Robert Cialdini. I plan to relate them to real-world examples and demonstrate how you can take advantage of them, no matter what your role, aim or goal in the negotiation is.

So, what are you waiting for? Your negotiation lowdown continues…

Chapter Three: Best Practices in Negotiation

"Start out with an ideal and end up with a deal."
Karl Albrecht

Now here's a question for you – are you a giver, a taker or a matcher? Whichever one you are, or which reciprocity style you veer towards, can determine how successful you are in negotiations.

Don't just take my word for it, take the word of Wharton professor and organizational psychologist Adam Grant. For the past 15 years, he has been teaching negotiation skills to the likes of Fortune 500 executives, U.S. Army and Air Force generals, and professional athletes in the NFL. These people expect results so you can bet he knows what he's talking about. (And who would want to go up against an Army general if you didn't?)

Grant's New York Times bestselling book, Give and Take, has helped to revolutionize traditional thinking around negotiation and defines the three exchange styles above, the giver, taker and matcher. So, which one are you?

Defining Givers, Takers and Matchers

Givers: As the name suggests, givers often give more than they get; they like to help others, even potentially at a cost to themselves. Grant points out that givers don't necessarily give money or volunteer for causes, but they like to help others by giving advice, making introductions and sharing knowledge. And they do so with no strings attached.

Takers: Takers see the world as a competitive place and look out for themselves. They may help others, but usually only if the benefits to them personally are greater than the costs. Takers often believe that for them to win, others must lose, what is known as a 'zero-sum game'.

Matchers: It's interesting to note that very few of us are 100% givers or 100% takers, we tend to hover somewhere between the two. That would make us a matcher. Matchers – most often seen in the workplace – are willing to exchange favors but usually on a quid pro quo basis, careful not to be exploited. They like to balance taking and giving, often keeping score to make sure everything is just and fair.

Do you recognize yourself in any of the above? The truth is that each of us can utilize all these styles at different times. We can be a giver in marriage, for instance, a matcher when sharing information with a co-worker, or a taker during a job interview negotiation. That said, we presumably lean more towards one than the other styles by nature.

To Be Successful, Which Should You Be....
Here's the kicker through – which one of these styles would you assume to be the most and least successful in life, career and negotiation?

Let me guess: you assume givers would be at the bottom of the pile, correct? Generous to a fault but too altruistic to get ahead in life. According to Grant's research, that's true. Givers really need to be careful not to become doormats and put everyone else's needs in front of their own.

But who is at the top, which style is the most successful? If you'd guess takers or matchers, you'd be in good company; most people assume these two styles will come out ahead… but you would also be WRONG.

According to Grant's research, it's the givers who are both at the bottom AND the top of the success pile. This applies across all industries too, from sales to medicine, to engineering and more.

Why? Because givers can build the most supportive networks, inspire their colleagues and achieve the most success in negotiations… if they steer clear of being pushovers. The most successful salespeople, for instance, are those who put their customers first.

"Being a giver is not good for a 100-yard dash, but it's valuable in a marathon."
Adam Grant

Give and Take – A Revolutionary Approach to Success

Most cultures and communities value giving. It's why doctors, teachers and other service-oriented people are held in such high esteem.

The irony is that it could be the matchers who have the most influence on who is successful.

Grant theorizes that the success and failure of takers and givers are heavily influenced by the matchers. Matchers want a fair and just world and can't stand to see takers winning by taking advantage of other people. So, matchers punish takers, perhaps by spreading rumors to damage their reputation. On the other hand, matchers want givers to be recognized and push for them to receive accolades, going out of their way to promote and support them.

I find this whole concept of givers, takers and matchers fascinating, but you may be asking yourself what it means for you. How can you learn from it to become better at negotiation?

Well, the reason I mention it at all is that Grant's research into givers, takers and matchers has led him to make some valuable suggestions for the negotiating room, which I'm going to share with you. Some of his negotiating tips go against established thinking, but that makes them more interesting, not less… and potentially more useful.

Along with social psychologist and Columbia Business School professor Adam Galinsky, who also works in this field, Grant suggests the following:

Best Practices to Follow in a Negotiation

Share Information
I know, I know, we're usually told to play our cards close to our chest in important negotiations, but here's where Grant's research into the three reciprocity styles wins out. Remember that, according to Grant, most people tend to be matchers, meaning there's a good chance that your opposite negotiating number, or a great many people in the room, will be also. These people will respond in kind to how we treat them, wanting to match us.

If we want trust, we must first give it.

In addition, studies also show that volunteering some information – it doesn't even have to be related to the negotiation – helps to make success more likely.

A 2002 experiment, for instance, asked Stanford and Northwestern students to negotiate over email. Those who revealed personal information about themselves, such as their hometown or hobbies, reached an agreement 59% of the time. This compares favorably to those straight-laced 'business-only' students who struggled to make agreements 40% of the time.

Making yourself a 'real person' in the other negotiator's eyes by sharing your hobbies, dreams or concerns often sets a conducive tone to positive negotiation.

Keep your Options Open
Good negotiators know beforehand what they want to get out of a negotiation, usually centered around several key issues. Inexperienced and experienced negotiators alike, however, often fall into the trap of sequencing their goals, believing they must come to an agreement on one topic before moving onto another.

So, they work at resolving salary, for instance, before moving onto other issues, such as vacation time, signing bonus or location. The problem with this step-by-step approach is that it can falter at any stage, leaving you unable to carry on. If you fail to agree on salary up front, for instance, you may never reach discussions on location, bonus or vacation time.

Skilled negotiators, in contrast, leave all the issues on the table, says Grant, citing researcher Neil Rackham. Doing so, gives you the *"flexibility to propose trading location and bonus for a bump in salary,"* writes Grant. Alternatively, if you can't agree on a salary, perhaps you can ask for more vacation time, or a bigger signing bonus, for instance. That may be something the hiring manager can agree to and may make enough of a difference for you to accept the offer.

By being transparent about all the issues on the table, both parties can compare their rankings and decide what's important to them. An agreement may finally come in the form of trade-offs in scope or requirements, for instance, if the client cannot reach your price.

Know Your Reservation and Target Prices
Make the First Offer
Social psychologist and Columbia Business School professor Adam Galinsky recommends you know both your walkaway price or terms (which he calls your reservation price) as well as your target price before any negotiation. Knowing your reservation price (the lowest you would accept) enables you to avoid accepting poor deals and helps to anchor the deal's value in your mind.

Both he and Grant also agree that making the first offer – traditionally shunned in negotiation– helps you to reach better terms in the end. They point out that research demonstrates the success of this unusual move, which takes advantage of the psychological principle of anchoring.

You see, once that first offer is on the table, it sets the stage and both negotiators begin to work around it, often without even realizing it. It's rare that an initial first offer is rejected out of hand; instead, it becomes the basis for further negotiation. The closer your first offer is to your target, therefore, the more likely you are to achieve it. Galinsky suggests that negotiating a salary is like selling a house: a higher initial offer usually leads to a higher final settlement.

If you're in a hiring situation, for instance, the hiring manager may say the figure is too much and lower it slightly, but that's typically still a better position to be in than if you start low and try to negotiate up. Whether or not they say your opening offer is ridiculous, they have still unconsciously been anchored and will feel the need to work around the figure, rather than rejecting it completely.

> *"When the final result is expected to be a compromise, it is often prudent to start from an extreme position."*
> **John Maynard Keynes**

Which brings me to another key point - don't be afraid to make an aggressive first offer. Most of us shy away from doing so because we fear to scare the other party away, but anchoring encourages us to look for data to support the offer, rather than reject it. A higher price, for instance, makes us look for the positives in a deal or product, while a lower one makes us look for the downsides.

Think of what you naturally do when browsing a luxury high-end apartment. The high associated price encourages you to look for the positives (concierge, security, location, furnishings) to back up the charge, doesn't it? In contrast, when looking at cheaper low-end houses, you can easily become fixated on the negatives (poor location, poor structure); in fact, you tend to look for them first to explain the low cost. Whether we know it or not, we do tend to live true to the 'you get what you pay for' ethos.

An aggressive first offer also gives you wiggle room to offer concessions and still reach an agreement.

Note that if you are unable to make the first offer, you need to counter the anchoring effect yourself. The best way to do that, suggests Grant, is to re-anchor. Let the other side know their offer is way off, and suggest a new figure, using the same information you would have used if you'd got the chance to make the first offer.

You could also use phrases to redirect the conversation, such as 'you may have been trying to test my thoughts with that first offer, but this is more what I had in mind...'

Making Counter Offers

"A miser and a liar bargain quickly."
Greek proverb

Everyone loves counter offers. It makes both sides feel as if they've pushed a hard bargain and got a good deal. Galinsky even suggests you don't take the first offer, no matter how perfect it may seem, but go back and ask for concessions to improve both participants' satisfaction levels.

Both of you will work harder and be more committed if you feel that you earned the results.

Demons that Ruin Negotiation
Grant and Galinsky's tips are great for in the boardroom or negotiating room, but you need to make sure you don't ruin your achievements by letting the negotiation demons into the room too. These are more personality-led and need to be checked in at the door. I'm talking about letting your emotions get the better of you, failing to listen, letting your ego take over and more.

The Importance of Listening
We've all done it. Have you ever tried so hard to persuade someone to your way of thinking, but the more information you give them and the better the arguments you make, the less interested they seem to become? It's frustrating, isn't it?

The hard truth, however, is that the problem lies not in them but in you; you are trying to persuade them using the wrong body part. (Ahem, this book will not take a turn, don't worry).

What you should be using instead of your mouth are your ears. (See? All perfectly innocent).
If you want to persuade anyone of anything, you'd be better to listen fully to them first. Talk less, listen more, ask revealing 'how' and 'what' questions – 'what do you think about….' 'how do you feel about…' – to learn more about them if you need to.

Why? Because there's more chance your co-workers, child, significant other, boss or whoever you're trying to persuade will listen to you if you listen to them.

I mean really listen to them, by the way, not just pretend to while eagerly awaiting an opportunity to barrage them with information anyway. Persuasion needs a relaxed and open participant and listening to someone encourages that. Besides, persuasion is far easier and more effective when you know what matters to the other person.

Likewise, people prefer to be persuaded by someone they like. Disagreeing, riding roughshod over people, not listening to them turns the other person off you. Agreeing with them, however, makes you seem agreeable, validates the other person and encourages them to continue the conversation. It also makes you more likable.

As far back as 1957, psychologist Leon Festinger defined cognitive dissonance to explain the discomfort people feel when people disagree and agree with them. If you're agreeable, I will like you more. The more I like you, the more likely I am to listen to you, and the better the negotiation will go.

<u>Beware Ego-Creep</u>

"Your ego is writing checks your body can't cash."
Top Gun

Ok, so there probably wasn't much that Tom Cruise couldn't do in Top Gun, making the above quote irrelevant, but for us mere mortals, ego-creep is a genuine concern.

Ask Canadian author, former cabinet minister and visiting professor, David Dingwall, about ego. In his book, *Negotiating So Everybody Wins*, he recalls his first time representing the Liberal government over funding with legendary United Mine Workers' representative William 'Bull' Marsh, back in 1981.

Clearly intimidated but determined to make an impression, Dingwall missed no opportunity to demonstrate his knowledge of the facts wherever possible in their first negotiations. Thinking he'd done a good job, he was shocked when Marsh raked him over the coals for not listening. His words, minus expletives, were something like *"When you speak, I listen. So next time when I talk, you better listen."*

Dingwall's error? Ego-creep. *"If you are thinking just of yourself, then you're in trouble,"* he says.

Top negotiators interviewed in his book concur. They stress that anyone who thinks they are the expert on a subject will appear arrogant, and the other side will respond in kind. This automatically rules out a good negotiating position, often making others want to flee the negotiating room as opposed to sitting down with you.

Avoid ego-creep by putting the deal or mandate first, rather than your own need to impress. Watch your language too. You'll be surprised at how much people are willing to bend over backward to work with someone who is likable. Great deals can be forged from humble questions, such as 'Could we try it this way?' or 'Would it be possible to remove X, Y and Z, and lower this rate?'

As author and entrepreneur Tim Denning says, *"In any business negotiation, the person with the bigger ego always loses in the long term".*

That's partly because a big ego blocks the ability to listen. We learn in life by listening to other people; it begins in childhood but continues throughout the decades. If you think you know everything, however, you stop listening, meaning you also stop learning as well.

Be humble, realize you don't know even a fraction of what there is to learn about yourself, other people and the world. Be open and flexible to new experiences and life lessons and let yourself grow.

Your negotiation style will improve drastically as a result, I promise you. The other negotiation demons include:

How To Not Show Neediness

Beware of showing neediness… it can sink a negotiation every time. Many years ago, I was looking to buy a one-bedroom apartment in a village in South East London. It wasn't a particularly cheap area, but it had greenery and wide-open spaces, something I craved being from a small village in Yorkshire myself. And something which is relatively hard to find in London. It also helped that my village was hip and popular, and I'd been renting there for a few years already.

I had my heart set on buying there, but it seemed as if I just couldn't afford anything nice. I looked at bedsits, one-bed apartments, both near the village and within walking distance of it. I saw apartments with mold, with black toilets, with not even enough room to swing a cat. I was down-hearted and wondering if I would have to move out.

Then I saw IT.

The perfect apartment, ground floor in a picturesque turn-of-the-century building, renovated inside to have all the mod cons. An open kitchen-diner, a big living room, decent-sized bedroom and room in the bathroom for a shower and a bath. (Trust me, that's also hard to find in one-bed apartments in London). Even better, it was just in my price range, albeit at the top end.

I fell in love, there and then. I knew this had to be my first proper apartment. I'm sure we've all been there, haven't we? Buying a house is such an emotional journey; I can never look at property with pure logic, I must feel it as well.

Luckily, I took a friend with me who was much better at negotiation in those days than I. He saw my eyes light up, knew exactly what I was thinking, and hissed at me to 'be quiet!' before I gave the game away.

I had to stand there, biting my lip, trying not to do a merry jig, while my friend dispassionately negotiated for the place on my behalf. He played it perfectly.

Yes, I was interested, he said, (good property goes so fast in London, there's no point messing around), but only at the right price. After all, it needed a bit of work doing, such as x, y and z. (For the benefit of those not in the room at the time, those things were minor, and I hadn't even noticed them). Plus, it involved a 10-minute walk to the train station, so it wasn't in the center of the village. (Again, he failed to mention that the walk was along the Heath, a beautiful piece of greenery, lifting the spirits before getting to work).

Me? I would have opened my purse and given him all the small change I had (as well as the asking price) if it helped.

We put in an offer below the asking price (something I would have been too afraid to do in case it was rejected) and there and then it was accepted! Within a couple of months, I owned my very first apartment, and how much did I love it!

I'm still grateful to my friend to this day for negotiating on my behalf. There was no way I wouldn't have telegraphed my neediness loud and clear, had I tried to do it myself.

This is key in negotiation; you need to exercise restraint. Distinguish between your emotional reaction and your logical one. If you can't, the other side will recognize your neediness and adapt accordingly by increasing the price, adding on a few additional charges or refusing to negotiate concessions… all because they know you'll buy it regardless.

I know I would have bought the apartment at the asking price or even increased it to compete with other interested parties if I had to.

(Funny how there are often other interested parties when you make it obvious that you're desperate to buy). As it was, my calm, dispassionate friend ensured I didn't need to… and I still had some money left over for decorating and buying furniture.

That was my first lesson, many years ago, in hiding neediness in negotiations, and it's still a rule I live by now, as a much more experienced negotiator. You'd do well to live by it too.

Bias
Bias can also be a sticking point in negotiation. We all have bias, perhaps against a person or an issue, but we need to be open to contrary information and actively listen to the other side. Ensure you're not just trying to confirm your own bias. Sticking to a first impression can anchor us too early in the negotiation, leaving us little room to maneuver.

Assumptions
You know what they say about making assumptions, so don't be an ass. Check your own and the other side's assumptions, verify all. One key element to clarify at the beginning of a negotiation is whether the person you're negotiating with has the authority to make decisions or promises. Does he or she have a mandate to do so, or must they go back to a superior before anything can be agreed upon? You'll need to adapt your negotiating style or expectations depending on the answer.

Controlling Emotions such as Anger and Anxiety

Alison Wood Brooks, Assistant Professor at Harvard Business School, has a great point to make about the role of anger in a negotiation.

Every year she sets her MBA students a task – to re-negotiate a fictitious strained deal between a supplier and client. The pair signed contracts eight months ago but are now at odds over terms. Each student assumes the position of client or supplier, is given confidential information about the company's policies and finances and is then tasked with renegotiating the deal.

That's not all, however. Some students are also secretly given another task… to be angry at the start of negotiations. They must feign anger for 10 minutes (finger-wagging, interrupting, calling the other party unreasonable) … all designed to examine how anger impacts negotiations.

Writing in the Harvard Business Review, Brooks says: *"As the pairs negotiate, I walk around and observe. Although some students struggle, many are spectacularly good at feigning anger… I've never seen the exercise result in a physical confrontation—but it has come close. Some of the negotiators who did not get the secret instructions react by trying to defuse the other person's anger. But some react angrily themselves—and it's amazing how quickly the emotional responses escalate."*

At the end of the task, some of the students are still arguing with one another. Once clued into the sub-text, however, it becomes clear to all… the more emotion displayed in a negotiation, the less likely it was to end well. Says Brooks: *"Bringing anger to a negotiation is like throwing a bomb into the process, and it's apt to have a profound effect on the outcome."*

Negotiation research used to focus primarily on strategies and tactics; it's only in the past decade or so that psychologists have begun to study the impact of different emotions on a negotiation. Research shows that looking anxious, for instance, can result in a poorer negotiation, so anyone feeling anxious would do well to mask it.

Anxious people tend to make lower offers, react quickly to counteroffers and try to exit the negotiations early, often agreeing to less financially attractive deals to do so.

Angry negotiators, meanwhile, escalate conflict and competitiveness, decrease co-operation, and make offers more likely to be rejected. It also damages long-term trust.

Controlling your emotions, therefore, is the first step towards a potentially positive negotiation.

I'll leave the last word to Brooks, who concludes: *"Good negotiators need to develop a poker face—not one that remains expressionless, always hiding true feelings, but one that displays the right emotions at the right times."*

Lady Ga-Ga would agree.

Chapter Four: Negotiation For ALL

"Let every eye negotiate for itself and trust no agent"
William Shakespeare

All the way back in chapter one, I mentioned that negotiation by women – or rather a lack of it – has been cited as a worrying problem by experts. Women's reluctance to negotiate is costing them millions in lost income over their lifetime.

Katie Donovan, the founder of consultancy Equal Pay Negotiations, warns that only 30% of women bother to negotiate annually for better compensation packages, compared to 46% of men. That accounts for almost $2 million dollars in lost income over a lifetime for an average woman wanting to climb the ladder.

The reticence strikes older and younger women alike.

Millennial career networking site, Levo, for instance, states that while 83% of its female members surveyed recognize how important salary/ benefits negotiation is when starting a new job, only 41% of them negotiated in their last job.

Let me put that in a different way. More than three-quarters of millennial women recognize they will earn less money throughout their career if they do not negotiate opening offers. They also appreciate that they will feel rewarded for their work by doing so.

And yet… more than half of them didn't negotiate in their last job. Why? According to Levo, it's because they didn't know how to ask for more (66%). A similar number (63%) felt uncomfortable negotiating, with more than half (58%) afraid of losing their job offer if they did ask for more.

Pretty staggering figures, aren't they? What sort of message is the working world sending women if they fear to lose a job offer for daring to speak out and ask for their worth? And why is this still happening in 2018?

Let me break off from my ire for a second to send a quick message to any men reading this – please don't think this chapter isn't relevant to you. It is. Both sexes need to work together to combat the gender pay gap and encourage fair negotiation.

"I hope the fathers and mothers of little girls will look at them and say 'yes, women can'" **Dilma Rousseff, Brazilian Statesman**

On a more selfish note, a lot of the tips I give here will be suitable for men too. It's not just women who are reluctant to negotiate. After all, I'm assuming it's one of the reasons the males reading, picked up this book. And let's look again at some of those figures mentioned above.

Yes, more men than women may negotiate annual job increases, but according to Katie Donovan above, that figure still only stands at 46%. Meaning that MORE THAN HALF of men don't ask for more or negotiate with their bosses.

Are you one of them? If so, keep reading. The rest of this chapter may focus primarily on women, but we have some potentially life-changing tips suitable for both sexes at the end.
Let's examine the issues and reasons women don't negotiate…

Negotiation Fail #1

As we already know, women are less likely than men to take the opportunity to negotiate when it arises. We are more likely to assume a proposal is definitive, whereas a man might chance a challenge anyway. This gender difference even extends to the U.S. Tennis Open Championships, where research showed women tennis players were 80% less likely to challenge a call made by the umpire than their male counterparts.

Linda Babcock, author of Women Don't Ask, created an experiment with colleagues Deborah Small and Michele Gelfand that demonstrates this reluctance perfectly.

Male and female students from Carnegie Mellon were recruited to play three rounds of the game Boggle and were told they would be paid between three and 10 dollars to take part. In the end, they were given three dollars, and asked, 'Here's three dollars. Is three dollars okay?"

The perfect opening to ask for more, wouldn't you think? Indeed, anyone who did ask for more money outright was given the full 10 dollars, no questions asked. Those students who just complained, however, or failed to ask for the money directly, were left with only three dollars.

Both sexes believed they'd played the game equally well, and both sexes complained equally about the payment. But, when it came to the crunch, almost NINE times as many men as women asked for more money.

Unhappy with what they were offered, men tried to fix it by asking for more, theorized Babcock. The women didn't do that.

"Women are the largest untapped reservoir of talent in the world"
Hillary Clinton

The 'fear' of negotiating affects women at all levels in all industries, even A-list Hollywood superstars aren't immune, as Jennifer Lawrence proved.

Writing for Lena Dunham's newsletter Lenny, Lawrence talks about the fallout from a 2014 email hack of Sony Pictures that revealed she was paid significantly less than her male American Hustle co-stars.

She wrote: *"I didn't get mad at Sony. I got mad at myself. I failed as a negotiator because I gave up early. "I would be lying if I didn't say there was an element of wanting to be liked that influenced my decision to close the deal without a real fight. I didn't want to seem* 'difficult' or 'spoiled'. At the time, that seemed like a fine idea, until I saw the payroll on the internet and realized every man I was working with definitely didn't worry about being 'difficult' or 'spoiled'."* Isn't that the truth?!

Fired former Sony co-chair Amy Pascal was responsible for those emails. Of the gender pay gap, she told Tina Brown at Women In the World San Francisco: *"The truth is that what women have to do is not work for less money. They have to walk away. People shouldn't be so grateful for jobs…People should know what they're worth and say no."*

She has a point, doesn't she? Granted, the troubles of an A-list actress who earned $52 million in one year alone or a fired Sony exec may not resonate with you, but when you're negotiating for your own humbler salary, it may help to think of Pascal's point above.

She also stresses that when you're running a business, it's not in your interests to encourage people to ask for more money. So, you don't. That doesn't mean that you don't expect other people to ask, however.

Negotiation Fail #2

As we know, there's a significant pay gap between men and women, and here's one potential reason… women aren't asking for a high enough salary. According to Hired, a digital job search platform, the average woman expects $14,000 less annually than her male counterparts.

The report, examining more than 100,000 job offers from 3,000 companies to 15,000 candidates, concluded that 63% of the time, men received higher offers than women… and let me reiterate, that's for the same job title at the same company.

Hired found that on average, women were offered 4% less than their male counterparts, but in some cases, the gap was as much as 45%. Is it blatant sexism; men preferring to pay other men more than women? But what if the hiring manager was a woman? Chances are some of that gap, if not the majority, comes about because women just aren't asking for the same money. And isn't it time women did?

If women don't challenge their initial pay offers, it all adds to the gender wage gap... and starts the female worker off on a lower salary than she truly deserves. That then becomes a problem that may plague her throughout her career.

Negotiation Fail #3

Yes, I know it sounds sexist and stereotypical, but experts now suggest that the way women are brought up, their 'socialization', is likely another of the remaining reasons for the gender pay gap.

Waverly Deutsch, a clinical professor at the University of Chicago's Booth School of Business, talks about the gender gap to The Atlantic. *"What's really interesting now is the role that women's socialization and how women approach their careers ... is one of the elements that might cause that gap to be persisting and make that last part of the gap harder to close."*

What does she mean by socialization? She's talking about the way we raise girls and women as opposed to boys and men. Men are raised to be masculine, not to show their emotions, to be aggressive, to confront danger, endure pain and to protect their loved ones.

Women, in contrast, are traditionally raised to be the nurturers, to be responsible, to be the caretakers. Why does that make a difference to their careers and salary? Possibly because girls are raised to be risk-averse, a preparation for the nurturing role of motherhood. Likewise, all too often women must choose between career and family; it's not always possible to have it all.

As *The Confidence Gap* from Katty Kay and Claire Shipman concludes, stereotypes, societal conditioning and expectations only serve to hold women back. Rightly or wrongly, there are perceptions at work that color how we view women's negotiation prowess.

Men are competitive, encouraged to be confident and go after what they want. Women, however, are classed as pushy or unnecessarily aggressive if they do the same. For some reason, women are not supposed to talk about money, and it makes many of us uncomfortable to do it, even those on the other side of the table.

In her book Own It, former Merrill Lynch CEO Sallie Krawcheck says: *"I hate making job offers; even after all these years and all the job offers I've made, I still have an almost physical aversion to doing it, for the fear that the other person will "get mad" at me that the compensation isn't generous enough. I know...seriously, right?"*

Negotiation Fail #4

I've hired quite a few people in my time, though probably nowhere near as many as Ms. Krawcheck above (and I'd bet on significantly smaller salaries as well). The one thing that strikes me now that I didn't appreciate before is that I can't remember a single woman I employed asking for more money on the initial offer. Not even one. A few men, yes, but no women.

I always put it down to the fact that jobs in our field were very competitive and they were glad of the offer. It makes me a little sick now to think that perhaps some of them worried I would rescind the offer if they asked for more. I hope I would have respected anyone of either sex who negotiated for more money, recognizing their bravery. (Of course, it doesn't mean I would have acquiesced! I'm a tough negotiator too).

Yet there is research out there that suggests women who choose not to negotiate, do so because they fear the 'social cost of negotiation'. That's essentially how they are viewed after negotiating for a pay rise or a better starting salary, i.e., how willing people are to work with the employee after seeing him or her negotiate.

Repeated studies show that while it is possible for men to alienate potential bosses, in most cases the social cost of negotiating is higher for women than for men, with female negotiators often penalized while men weren't.

Male hiring managers were less keen to work with women who negotiated, for instance, whereas their opinion of the men who did so didn't change. (The exception to this is a study with a female hiring manager who penalized anyone who tried to negotiate, man or woman. Equal opportunity bias, at least!)

It may seem harsh to label this a negotiation fail, as it's a real and proven issue. You may believe it's understandable then that many women choose not to negotiate. But here's the rub… if women choose not to negotiate because they fear how people will judge them, the situation will never change or improve.

The only thing that can alter this perception and social cost of negotiation is for more women to negotiate and to normalize it. Of course, it would help if hiring managers checked their bias in at the door too, men and women alike.

If we allow the situation to continue, we do ourselves as women a great disservice. Men, this is an issue for you as well. We are all someone's wife, daughter, sister, mother, friend…

So, let's assume that we, as women, want to negotiate. Many men share our reticence or lack of negotiation experience too, so how can we all improve? How can we find the confidence to ask for what we are worth? Very few businesses are going to offer more money from the goodness of their hearts. You're going to need to ask for it and to make a good argument while you're doing it.

Finding the Confidence to Negotiate

"A woman is like a tea bag - you can't tell how strong she is until you put her in hot water"
Eleanor Roosevelt

Carol Sankar, founder of The Confidence Factor for Women, shares a few tips to help us find the confidence to negotiate. While she intended them as advice for women, they work for everyone.

<u>Negotiation shouldn't just be about money:</u> ask for new responsibilities or roles to help you make the most of your skills or learn new ones. It's often the best way to an increase in compensation as well later down the line, as you'll increase your worth to the company.

<u>Keep the personal out of it:</u> Yes, you may be rejected the first (or second) time you ask, but it's usually not personal. It's often about the budget and the bottom line. Improve your argument the next time and demonstrate your worth to the boss.

<u>Know your unique contribution to the company:</u> what do you bring to it, what would the corporate culture miss if you had to be replaced? Focus on being an asset, not just an employee.

Number One Tip: Negotiate for Others

Research has proven that women are better at negotiating for others. Harvard Professor Kathleen McGinn who has researched negotiation noted that negotiation is 'demasculinized' when women worked for a group as opposed to working for themselves.

This can be relevant to men too, who struggle to represent themselves in negotiations adequately.
In his book Give and Take, Adam Grant tells the story of Sameer, an Indian man, ranked in the top 10% of northeast United States employees in his firm and a star performer.

Sameer liked to help and mentor younger employees, but despite being one of the most valued people in his company, he missed out on promotions and well-deserved salary raises on a regular basis. Why? Because he never asked for them. In Sameer's own words, *"I did not want to make others uncomfortable or overstep my bounds."*

Sameer, whose father was born into poverty but clawed his way up to middle class, had been shielded as a child and never learned how to negotiate. Later, his wife did the negotiating for him, and he let her. He admits to being ashamed of his submissiveness but seemed unable to change it. Until, one day, he did. He asked his Fortune 500 company for a higher salary and reimbursement for tuition too.

He got his request, plus he earned the respect of his boss who was impressed by his assertiveness.

So, what changed? How did Sameer find the courage to negotiate, and to do so in a strong fashion? The answer is simple, but oh so effective. He began to negotiate on behalf of other people and not himself.

It's a technique that has been proven to work. Grant quotes an experiment by Women Don't Ask author Linda Babcock and colleagues, who recruited 176 senior executives with titles such as CEO and COO, President, Chairman, General Manager etc… Each had to play the role of an employee in a software company who was being promoted and had to negotiate compensation/ salary, perks and conditions.

Babcock found that the male execs landed a salary on average 3% higher than the female executives. BUT when they told the participants that they were now negotiating on behalf of a mentee, the women then earned salaries on average 14% HIGHER than the men. When the women advocated for someone else, they pushed harder to reach their goals.

Several other studies back up these findings. On average, male executives landed the same salaries regardless of whether they were advocating for themselves or someone else. Female execs, however, tended to do much better when they negotiated for other people than when they did it for themselves.

It's an effective technique that reluctant negotiators of any gender can use. Sameer's inspiration was his family; he began to negotiate for them.

Grant quotes Sameer as saying: *"The solution was thinking about myself as an agent, an advocate for my family… I feel guilty about pushing too much, but the minute I start thinking, 'I'm hurting my family, who's depending on me for this,' I don't feel guilty about pushing for that side."*

So, the next time you need to negotiate, remind yourself of everyone relying on you at home – significant other, children, dogs, cats, budgie, goldfish… whatever you need to give you the confidence to advocate. And go ahead and do it!

Chapter Five: Introducing the Six KEY Principles of Persuasion

So far in this book, I've focused on giving you the drive and the confidence you need to negotiate whatever you want and suggested some techniques to help you do that. From setting the scene to learning the fundamental rules of negotiation, to warning you of negotiation demons to avoid… it's been a learning curve, hasn't it?

Now it's time I give you the tools you need to persuade. You see, at its heart, negotiation is all about persuasion.

It's how you present your ideas in such a way that encourages the other person to agree with you and to act. Note that I said the way you present your ideas… and didn't say anything about the ideas themselves.

Yes, of course, I'd hope your ideas or the products you sell are well thought out and value-added – indeed in the longer term you are unlikely to succeed if they're not – but for our current purposes, that's not the key focus. It's the way you communicate the benefits that can make the difference between success and failure, between persuading someone to do what you want or not.

There is a science behind persuasion, one that researchers have been studying for years. Simply put, there are techniques you can employ to 'get people to yes'.

You may foolishly believe that people consider all relevant information before coming to a decision, but you'd be wrong (and bless you, but a little naive too). In today's overloaded world, we're always searching for shortcuts, and it's no different when it comes to making decisions.

You could say that we look for 'rules of thumb' to speed up the decision-making process, things that mostly worked before, so we'll keep doing them. If we've already agreed to give to a charity, for instance, we're likely to agree to do so again, and we'll do it without thinking much about it. That's known as the consistency principle, the desire to stick to our decisions, according to the 'Godfather of influence', Dr. Robert Cialdini.

Or perhaps we trusted a celebrity's recommendation of a brand before and it worked well, so we're more likely to do it again and without much question. That's the Authority Principle.

Dr. Cialdini, the New York Times best-selling author of Influence: Science & Practice and Pre-Suasion: A Revolutionary Way to Influence and Persuade, has spent his entire career researching the science of influencing, and he has identified six such shortcuts to persuasion. They are: Reciprocity, Scarcity, Authority, Consistency, Liking and Consensus.

The key to each one of these is that done correctly, they can bypass the conscious mind and trigger an unconscious reaction. You see something is scarce, for instance, and it automatically makes you want it more. You probably don't even know why it's just that instinctual.

The useful thing about the above is that knowing how these 'rules of thumb' operate enables us to take advantage of them, ethically of course.
This is true whether you want to persuade someone to buy a product, service, or to invest in yourself. Which is why this chapter will touch on marketing and sales, as well as selling yourself at the office or in a job interview.

Let's look at each one of the Six Principles of Persuasion, in turn, to see how we can make them work for us….

Persuading People to Say Yes

The Principle of Reciprocity

The principle of reciprocity is as simple as it is effective. From childhood, we're taught to repay the kindness of others – we feel obliged to return dinner invitations, to owe colleagues a favor if they do one for us, to buy a round of drinks if our friend does it first. We don't want to feel indebted.

This psychological trigger works in business too. In short, people are more likely to say yes to people who they owe or have an obligation towards.

Don't believe me? Let me ask you a question: are you a seasoned restaurant-goer? If so, you might think you choose to tip (or not) depending on a whole host of things, such as quality of food, service, atmosphere, waiter's demeanor etc...

Surely you wouldn't be influenced by a little 'gift' like a chocolate when it comes time to pay, would you? According to research, yes you would!

Researchers Strohmetz, Rind, Fisher and Lynn examined the subject in their report Sweetening the Till. They demonstrated that offering a piece of chocolate or mint to diners significantly influences the tip given.

But here's where it gets interesting. The researchers wanted to test the theory that the tip size would increase in correlation to how much chocolate was given (one piece or two).

Diners were given two pieces of chocolate this time and the tip received as a result did indeed increase. But the manner in which the chocolate was offered was also a significant factor.
While tips increased when guests were given two chocolates on the plate (an increase of 14% according to Dr. Cialdini), it increased even further when the server personally gave the second round of chocolates to the diners, offering 'an extra chocolate just for you'. The increase? 23%. That could make a server's night. The personal touch ensured the diners felt more obligation, and tips increased as a result.

So, what's our takeaway from this? How can you use the principle of reciprocity to your advantage to encourage people to buy, to listen to you, to feel obliged to do what you want?

The useful thing to note here is that reciprocation doesn't have to be equal. You only need to offer some small token of kindness – an unexpected gift, an additional service, for instance – and people will feel obliged to return the favor. That's why reciprocity is a popular strategy in marketing, where companies offer free samples or charities offer small gifts. You can bet your bottom dollar that their research has told them it's worth the generosity.

So, how best can you utilize reciprocity?

How to Trigger Reciprocity

There are three key ways in which you can trigger reciprocity in marketing, for instance. They are:

Offer something first: people will feel obliged to respond

Make it unexpected or exclusive: this will make the recipient feel special

Personalise the offer: as we've seen by the additional tip, people appreciate the personal touch and will reward you for it.

Spotify's ad-free 30-day Premium membership trial is a great example of reciprocity: it can be canceled at any time with no cost and only costs $8 a month when the trial ends, meaning a lot of people simply don't cancel.

But can the principle of reciprocity help us in our negotiations for salary, or a job interview? Yes, absolutely. The beauty of it is that it can be used in any negotiation, even by people with no leverage, if correctly wielded.

Using Reciprocity in a Job Interview or Promotion Scenario

Reciprocity works best if you can make your negotiating counterpart feel indebted to you in some way.

If you are negotiating your annual salary, for instance, make it clear to your employer that you are making a concession or giving something away to engender the feeling of indebtedness. Point out how you have worked overtime for months without compensation and do so because you enjoy your job, but now it's only fair that you get some sort of compensation for it.

Be on the lookout for any opportunities for reciprocity in a job interview situation too. Perhaps you could make an unselfish gesture to the interviewer or hiring manager to encourage reciprocation. If you're an expert in one field, for instance, or have knowledge the other person doesn't, you could voluntarily share your expertise or cost-saving advice if it seems appropriate.

For example, if the hiring manager is talking about new software the company is thinking of investing in, you could say: "It's very good software for x, but when we used it at my old/ current job, we found x, y and z. You might find that for your purposes so-and-so is more appropriate. I can email you further information after this meeting if you'd like." By giving away your knowledge for free, you are creating a good feeling and vibe between you and the person interviewing you.

Alternatively, if you are negotiating a starting salary or benefits for a potential new job, demonstrate that you are willing to cooperate by making a gift or concession in the early stages of talks. You could do this by making an initial high but reasoned claim, putting you in a good position to make a concession in the next round.

The best way I can think of to adequately describe the principle of reciprocity in a negotiation over money is to revert to the car salesman and buyer story.

You are buying a car. The salesman wants £15,000 and you counter with £10,000. The seller then reduces his price to £13,000. What would you normally do in this situation? The seller has made a concession so, assuming you do want the car, you'd probably be tempted to put in a higher bid of, say, £12,000 and hopefully, you'd have a deal, with both sides happy.

You may assume you just 'played the game' but the reason you felt almost compelled to increase your bid was due to the principle of reciprocation. The seller had just made a concession to you and you wanted to acknowledge that.

The same works in salary negotiation too. Ask for a higher but reasoned salary bid expecting some negotiation, and when you later make your concession and reduce the request, the hiring manager or employer will acknowledge that and hopefully show some appreciation. The idea is to ask for a reasonable request but one that exceeds your true target, expecting to adjust down slightly until you come to an agreement – hopefully around your real target. The ideal concession will provide the employer with some benefits but will cause you little harm at the same time.

The Principle of Scarcity

When British Airways announced the end of their London to New York Concorde flights in 2003 because they just weren't economical, sales soared the very next day. Why did they suddenly become more popular? After all, the cost of tickets, service and length of the journey hadn't changed, only one thing had: the flights had become scarce.

As such, they became more desirable.

Make something scarce and we'll want it more. Why? Because we assume it's better. If something is scarce, we assume it's because more people want it. We therefore associate scarcity with quality.

If you're selling a product or negotiating a deal, trigger a sense of urgency and people will pay attention.

You can do this by:
Offering a limited number: the product or item is scarce because it's in short supply and won't be available after it runs out

Offering a limited time: the product or deal is on the table for a limited time, not available after that

Use competitions: By their nature, the item is scarce so encourage people to compete in auctions or bids.

Quick note: If you want to boost the effectiveness of the scarcity principle, make sure you also point out what's unique about your proposition and what people will lose if they don't take advantage of it. Research demonstrates that people are often persuaded more by what they might lose than what they will gain.

How to Use the Scarcity Principle in a Workplace Situation

In a workplace negotiation situation, use the scarcity principle to describe the unique advantages of any recommendation or offer you make, but be sure to tell the boss not only of the benefit they'd gain but what they would lose by not accepting your offer.

In an interview, you can use the scarcity principle by demonstrating how you are unique, scarce or valuable. Do this by identifying your unique points and addressing what you can bring to the organization that others can't. How will you add value to their company, or increase company profits, for instance?

Again, take advantage of the fear of losing: if they do not employ you, what will they miss out on? What will their rival gain if they hire you instead?

Once you've sold the potential employer on your relevant expertise and its value to their organization, you could start to hint at the idea that other people want you. Bring up other offers of employment and ask for details about the company's future and growth. Make sure you don't shoot yourself in the foot here, of course.

The idea is to stress to the employer that they should be lucky to have you and to take away the notion that you will be grateful for the job. It then becomes more of a negotiation and you have strength in future salary negotiations.

The Principle of Authority
Research demonstrates that we like to follow the lead of people who we perceive as credible or knowledgeable, experts if you will. After all, they have usually earnt their positions by virtue of impressive skill, knowledge or expertise in their area, probably more than most of us possess.

You can use that to your advantage by becoming an authority in your chosen field yourself and using that authority in a negotiation.

Of course, if you're hoping to persuade someone to follow your lead in a negotiation because of your expert credentials and authority, you must first demonstrate them, which can be the awkward part. You don't necessarily want to sit there reeling off your qualifications and expertise, so here are the factors that trigger the authority principle according to Dr. Cialdini.

Titles: Titles such as Prof, Ph.D., CEO, Chairman, Founder all display your authority up front. We can't possibly cross-reference and confirm everyone's credibility, so we've come to rely on job titles and other titles instead. You'll tend to find that 'experience-related' titles such as CEO and Director are more persuasive than education-related ones in certain areas, such as business and ecommerce.

Clothes: Clothes maketh the man, so they say, and the right look can certainly convey expertise. Uniforms are an obvious example, but suits can also demonstrate power and authority, as can the religious outfits of nuns, priests etc…

Trappings/ Symbols of Authority: Accessories can also offer indirect clues as to our authoritative or senior roles, such as a police badge, a doctor's white coat etc…

Some businesses have already cottoned on to the authority principle, giving its employees titles that engender trust and respect. Not all of the tech support that work in Apple's Genius Bars, for instance – a customer-facing role in all but one of Apple's stores – are likely MENSA-accredited geniuses, but the title encourages us to trust them for their expertise anyway.

This backs up research that tells us that we are likely to trust people for their authority if they display signs of it (via titles, trappings or clothes as mentioned above), and we will do so even if they do not actually have said authority. (Presumably, until they demonstrate their lack of it).

Now is not the time to be humble. Research shows that we must signal our authority and credentials to others before we attempt to influence them. So, if you have diplomas, hang them on your office walls. People are more likely to trust a physiotherapist, for instance, who has medical degrees or diplomas on his/ her wall than one who does not.

Likewise, if you're about to enter negotiations with someone, provide them with information about yourself first – articles about your achievements, LinkedIn profile, credentials, background information, anything that demonstrates your authority.
If it's not possible or appropriate for you to stress your expertise yourself, consider arranging for someone else to do it for you. It can prove equally as effective. Take this example from a group of estate agents, as quoted by Dr. Cialdini on his Influence at Work blog.

The estate agents/ real estate agents quoted managed to boost the number of property appraisals by 20% and subsequent contracts by 15%, all by having reception staff mention their credentials and expertise. For example, anyone ringing about lettings was told, *"Lettings? Let me connect you with Sandra, who has over 15 years' experience letting properties in this area."* Or, anyone calling for sales: *"Speak to Peter, our head of sales. He has over 20 years' experience selling properties."*

Having someone else testify to their credentials helped to establish their authority, meaning people were more likely to trust and follow them. Try it next time you need to persuade someone.

Using the Authority Principle in Job Interviews and Negotiations

Obviously, when it comes to a job interview, you want to demonstrate your authority to the interviewer. Don't just rely on your CV or resume to do it for you: that just got your foot in the door.

Build on your reputation throughout the interview by referring to blog posts and industry articles that you've written, share your knowledge on the sector with the employer, demonstrate how you can use it to benefit his or her company (Be specific, let them know how you can reduce overheads, win new contracts, boost productivity etc….). Aim to be seen as an expert by the interviewer and your answers will rarely be challenged.

I once went for a job interview for the launch editor of a new lifestyle website. As well as providing my resume, I did my homework and provided a 'sample' launch plan. The intention was to set myself up as an expert, both in the subject matter (lifestyle issues) and web launches. I also liberally dropped in references to 'when I set up x, y and z' throughout my interview and was at pains to offer concrete examples of my successes.

I'll admit that it was a bold move that could have backfired – I could have completely misread the tone or ethos of the company and come off as an arrogant know-it-all. My launch plan could have been rubbish, or they could have had alternative plans of their own that put mine to shame. Or they could have asked questions that I, as a self-confessed 'expert', couldn't answer. Wouldn't that have been embarrassing?!

Luckily, it turned out that my sample launch plan gave us something to talk about during the interview and allowed me to genuinely demonstrate my expertise and talents. They must have liked both because they offered me the job within 10 minutes of me leaving the building.

I don't say this to brag but to point out that if you don't take the opportunity to sell yourself and your expertise in a job interview, you're missing a trick. Don't hide your talents because you feel uncomfortable 'selling yourself'; your interviewer won't thank you for it.

The Principle of Consistency
This is sometimes called the commitment and consistency principle because, even though the two principles are different, they are closely related. The act of making a commitment encourages consistency.

Simply put, this shortcut to persuasion takes advantage of the desire to stick to what we know or to maintain a commitment we've already made. The principle of consistency occurs because people by nature want to stand by their prior opinions, actions, behavior or statements.

We're asked to make hundreds of decisions each day, aren't we, so it's no great surprise that we like to make a single decision and stick to it. Once we've made that decision, it becomes our reference point for all related choices in the future. We recall how we handled the situation in the past, and default to the same decision or behavior in the future. It's automatic, one reason why habits are so hard to break.

It's a great opening for customer loyalty too, of course.

Encourage people to commit to a particular stance, statement or identity and they'll feel an automatic compulsion to stand by it. Assuming the commitment was voluntary, to begin with. That's the critical bit. Choices made under coercion will not work. The decision should be self-motivated.

Charities, for instance, know that petitions rarely work but the act of getting you to voluntarily sign a petition on the charity's behalf works on you: you strengthen your belief in the charity because you put your name to it.

As Dr. Cialdini says: *"Once we have made a choice or taken a stand, we will encounter personal and interpersonal pressures to behave consistently with that commitment. Those pressures will cause us to respond in ways that justify our earlier decision."*

If you pay attention to the marketing and examples of persuasion around you, you'll notice that companies leverage the consistency principle all the time by:

<u>Encouraging public commitments:</u> When people commit to something in public, they are less likely to back out of it.

<u>Getting their foot in the door:</u> Savvy companies or charities rarely ask for the world at the start of the customer-client relationship (or employer-employee relationship); instead, they will look for, and ask for, small initial commitments. It's a simple concept. Ask for a small request that is easy to say 'yes' to. This commitment then triggers the consistency principle which makes it easier for people to say yes to further requests. Note that the more effort someone puts into a commitment, the more likely they are to be consistent.

Marketers take advantage of this concept when they offer free webinars. Unlike free content (useful for reciprocity), a webinar takes commitment, say an hour of your time. By making such a commitment, it makes it much more likely that we'll buy the product in the future because we'll want to stay consistent.

<u>Rewarding customers:</u> Reward your customers for their time and effort invested in your brand and it will reinforce their need for consistency. (While also triggering the reciprocity principle, well done!)

<u>The Secret:</u> Note that a verbal commitment increases the chances that someone will actually follow through with their pledge, but the real secret to success is to get someone to write it down. Once the customer or person you're negotiating with writes their commitment down – whether in a formal agreement or not –they are unlikely to change their minds. Combine this with active, voluntary and public commitments.

<u>Using the Consistency Principle in a Work or Interview Setting</u>
When you're negotiating with, say the boss for a promotion, the key is to recognize a prior commitment he or she made to you and link it to the current request. Ideally, that should trigger the principle of consistency, making him or her more likely to promote you if possible because they've invested in, and committed to, you already.

In a job interview situation, you might wonder how to create consistency. The key is to create a commitment towards you in the interviewer's mind first, which is, after all, the target of a job interview.

You could potentially do this by framing some of your interview questions as answers, designed to generate an interest in you and your skills. If asked what you achieved in your last job/s, for instance, you could say: *"In my last few companies, I reduced staff turnover and boosted morale by doing x, y and z."* Or *"I saved costs and boosted profitability by doing x, y and z."* And here's the kicker – you should then ask something like, *"Is that a strategy that could benefit your company?"*

The idea is to create commitment and consistency by getting the interviewer to repeatedly say he or she would benefit from your ideas throughout the interview. Once he or she commits to you in their mind, it will make it harder for them to change their mind due to commitment/ consistency principles.

The Principle of Liking

Lots of research tells us that people are more likely to say yes to people they like. In short, we are more easily influenced by people we like than by people we don't like. It makes sense, doesn't it? It's why we laugh at one person's joke because we like them but may feel offended if the same joke was told by someone we didn't.

It's that simple but also that complex, because how can we make people like us, especially if we don't have a lot of time to schmooze or if our negotiation is taking place online?

To make matters slightly more complex, the people we 'like' can vary from close friends to complete strangers that we are attracted to. It goes some way to explaining why word of mouth testimonials and recommendations from our peers or endorsements from famous actors, actresses and singers are so effective. It's one reason companies use well-known sports stars and respected celebrities as ambassadors for their brands.

So, how can we make people like us? According to the science of persuasion, there are three main factors that encourage people to like us. They are:
- We like people who seem similar to us;
- We like people who pay us compliments;
- We like people who work towards mutual goals with us.

Remember the Stanford and Northwestern study I mentioned in chapter three, where students negotiated online? Those who shared personal information about themselves (hometown or hobbies) before negotiating made a deal much more often than those who did not. That's thanks to the principle of liking.

We're all suckers for flattery, even if we suspect it's not genuine, and you'll find many salespeople use this tactic, even if they're not sure why it works. If we have a good opinion of ourselves, we're happy to accept the praise, which endears us to whoever delivered it.

If you're trying to persuade people to buy your product or service, there are several things you can do to boost your likeability factor. They include:

Encourage familiarity: Form relationships with your customers via social media, hold intimate conversations rather than just using the platform to broadcast. People tend to trust the familiar and the best way to do this is to have regular positive contact.

Consider it this way, if you spend two hours with someone, you'll get to know them a little. But spend the same amount of time split into 20 or 30-minute segments over a few weeks, and you'll probably feel that you know them even better. You're certainly more likely to feel positively towards them.

Well done, you have established a history, familiarity and comfort level with your customers that can be invaluable. Familiarity doesn't always breed contempt; in this case, it encourages a sense of security.

Be Similar: Demonstrate that you are a person behind your brand, act like a friend or someone your customers can relate to.

Cooperate: Fight for causes that mean something to your customers; the feeling of teamwork encourages rapport.

Associate: On the same note, associate your brand with others that share the same values, and/ or associate your brand with the values you want to communicate with your customers.

Be Attractive: This isn't as shallow as it sounds! While we do naturally tend to drift towards people we're attracted to and are more likely to respond to requests from, this also includes your brand and physical signs of. Design your website well, for instance, to suit your product or service, and ensure it functions well, and people will like it more.

Using the Liking Principle in Job Interviews and Similar Situations

At its most basic, we are more predisposed to like someone if they compliment us and if they smile, so make sure to be a 'person' in your job interview. By that I mean, don't be afraid to let your (ideally upbeat and friendly) personality shine through.

You need the interviewer to like you, otherwise, you'll never get the job. Respect their gut feelings – most interviewers are swayed by them – and increase the chance they'll like you by finding common ground.

Research the interviewer before you meet: did you go to the same university, do you play the same sport, have you worked with the same people? (Be careful not to criticise anyone you previously worked with).

The interviewer is likely to let slip some of their interests, hobbies and beliefs during the interview, so be on the lookout for those. If you can, demonstrate that you share the same beliefs, values and work ethic, or make it known that you have similar convictions.

Once the interviewer decides that he or she likes you, it will be the filter through which they will view the rest of the interview.

I think the best job interview I personally ever had, just beating the one I mentioned above, was with a woman who became my boss, close mentor and eventually a good friend.

It was quite a few years ago now and I was a nervous wreck before the interview. I was going for a job that I thought I would never get in a million years; I just wasn't sure I was qualified enough.

So, imagine my dismay when, a few hours before the interview, my head-hunter called me with some unexpected last-minute 'honesty'. She had just had a run in with my potential interviewer and wasn't in the best mood for a pep talk. As such, she felt that she had to warn

me that the woman was impossible to please, had turned down better candidates than me and that I would probably hate her.
Yes, I was shocked (very!) at her unprofessionalism as well, but in a way, she did me a favor.

I don't know what it says about me, but I thrived in that interview. Hearing that I couldn't possibly impress my interviewer anyway quelled my nerves and I went in there swinging (metaphorically, of course). And guess what? We hit it off.

My interviewer was just a few years older than me and we bonded over the idea of news/ current affairs and what it should and could be, online. We shared some of the same ideologies, had dealt with some of the same issues (women working in a mostly man's world) and we seemed to share a similar outlook on life (which if you asked me to describe, I'd say is no-nonsense 'just-get-on-with-it', with a bit of whimsy and romance thrown in).

I'd describe the interview as nothing less than a meeting of minds and I assume she felt the same because I, probably the poorer candidate on paper, got the job.

This 'disagreeable' woman, let's call her April to protect her privacy, became the best boss I'd ever had, a giving mentor and a friend to this day. Ironically, I learned later that we both had the same reaction to the head-hunter who put me forward for the job… we just couldn't get on with her at all!

The Principle of Consensus or Social Proof
At heart, we humans are social creatures. We look to other people and take our cues from them, to see how others behave and act in order to determine how we should. That's especially true in areas where we are uncertain.

Ever walked past an empty restaurant and chose a busier one instead on the basis that it must be better if more people are eating there? I certainly have. That's because we are inherently influenced by what other people are saying or doing, whether we want to be or not.

Dr. Cialdini reports on a hotel experiment to demonstrate the power of social proof. A hotel leaves a small card in bathrooms pointing out that reusing your towel can have environmental benefits… and 35% of guests reuse their towel and comply. A hotel notes that 75% of guests will reuse their towel at some point in a four-night stay and includes that information on the cards too. The result? Towel reuse rose by a further 33%.

The takeaway? If you want to persuade people, point to what other people, especially similar people, are already doing.

Consider the power of testimonials, for instance, they can make or break your business.

In it's 2017 Local Consumer Review Survey, investigating the power of consumer reviews on local businesses, BrightLocal discovered that nearly three-quarters of people (73%) trust a business more if it has positive reviews. Most people (85%) trust online reviews as much as personal recommendations, with customers reading an average of seven reviews before deciding whether to trust a business or not.

The key for your own business success, therefore, is to build up trust in your product or service. (Note, according to BrightLocal, the majority of people will leave an online review if asked).

It also makes sense that we will have more faith in things endorsed or popular with people that we trust, whether it's celebrities, peers or experts. Aim then for approval from:

<u>Credible experts in a relevant field</u>
<u>Paid or unpaid endorsements from celebrities.</u>
When Mark Zuckerberg posted on Facebook about grilling thermometer iGrill, for instance, the iGrill website crashed because it couldn't handle the interest. iGrill CEO Christopher Allen said downloads of their app 'exploded' following the unexpected mention.

Approval from the masses (the 'so many people can't be wrong' approach)
Past and present users (NB: 30% of people questioned by BrightLocal believe it is important for brands to respond to reviews, and will judge them accordingly). Peer review from friends and people the customer knows are also very important.

How to Use Social Proof in a Career or Job Interview Scenario
The best way to trigger the social proof principle is to create a buzz around yourself. If you want to be seen as an expert in a particular field, for instance, (perhaps one that has a project coming up in the medium future), keep dropping relevant information into your work conversations. Pepper your discussions with 'expert' information and when someone asks who has experience in this market, others will remember your knowledge and recommend you.

If that recommendation comes from someone the questioner trusts (i.e., another senior manager) or comes from multiple sources, it is more likely to be believed.

The same is true in a job interview scenario. Here you want to create that buzz around your expertise, but the key factor is that the praise shouldn't come from you. Self-praise or repeatedly telling the interviewer how wonderful you are will not trigger the social proof principle.

To do this, you need to create the buzz about yourself by quoting other people. Drop in comments about past employers praising you for your success, provide evidence from co-workers, bosses, stakeholders of their satisfaction working with you, repeat statistics detailing your successes, as listed by the management team etc....

The aim is to encourage the new employer to think 'If everyone else believes he is successful, I will too.'

You could also let slip that you have had other offers for similar positions from a couple of other established competitive companies.

So, there you go. Six proven techniques that can help you make small, practical changes to significantly improve your negotiation and persuasion skills. They are potentially so powerful because they bypass the rational mind, appealing to our subconscious.

As Joseph Murphy, author of The Power of Your Subconscious Mind, says: *"As you sow in your subconscious mind, so shall you reap in your body and environment."*

Trust me, it's pretty powerful stuff.

Chapter Six: Effective Negotiation in Professional or Serious Settings

Whether you're a CEO or a worker bee, a lawyer, doctor or a carpenter, you'll no doubt spend a significant proportion of your professional life negotiating.

It could be with clients, with other professionals, your team, other departments, the boss, with co-workers and/ or with customers… there's no denying that how effectively you negotiate can have a direct impact upon your personal career success and the future of the business.

The negotiation may be overt – different departments coming together to thrash out budgets, for instance – or covert, such as tackling personality clashes between team members. It can be structured (appraisals, salary and promotion requests) or on the hoof (fire-fighting unexpected client complaints).

One thing stands true for all of these types of negotiation… the stronger the negotiator you are, the better the results will be.

Being able to persuade others is a valuable skill that can translate into strong leadership, huge sales, promotions, salary raises and numerous other successes. But of course, you knew that, which is why you picked up this book.

Hopefully, by now, you've already learned many invaluable professional negotiation and persuasion tips. Let's do a quick recap of what we've learned so far.

In chapter one, we learned just how important negotiation skills are and how we use them every day, while in chapter two we jumped straight into how best to set the scene for an effective negotiation. (We're not sitting around twiddling our thumbs here, are we?!)

In chapter three, I shared Adam Grant's tips for best practices in the negotiation room, based around his astute observations of givers, takers and matches, while chapter four examined the curious differences between male and female negotiating styles and attitudes.

In chapter five, we got down to the six principles of persuasion – reciprocity, scarcity, authority, consistency, liking and consensus – and discussed how to use each to your benefit in job interviews, salary negotiations and other professional settings.

In fact, we've already discussed negotiation in a professional setting so much, what else can there possibly be to talk about?! You'd be surprised!

Before I go on to reveal the specific subjects for this chapter, however, let me issue an appeal: if you haven't yet read all of the chapters so far, please go back and do so.

You see, this book is intended to build upon your knowledge chapter by chapter. While you could skip straight to the 'good bits', you'd end up missing a whole lot of useful information in the meantime.

You could, for instance, jump straight into this chapter – Negotiation in a Professional Setting – and gain some useful insights, but be warned: **I'm not going to repeat the information I shared before.**

This is not a crib sheet, nor is it a quick fix.

Improving your negotiation skills takes genuine commitment, and that's why I've designed this book to work with you, and to build your knowledge chapter by chapter. Otherwise, it would be the same broad-brush approach that you could find everywhere, and I think you deserve more than that.

So, if you have skipped chapters, do yourself a favor and go back and read those first. Make sure you don't miss the bigger picture.

For now, allow me to focus on the broader aspects of negotiation in a professional setting that we haven't talked about in detail yet, such as how to establish trust and conversely, what to do if you don't trust the person you're negotiating with. Likewise, we'll talk about how to avoid falling victim to brinkmanship and what you should do if a negotiation fails.

But first, before we jump into the deeper issues, here's a conundrum for you. What can you do if you've found your dream job, but it doesn't come with a dream salary? If a pay bump is out of the question, can negotiation still save the day?

Now is the time to learn how to negotiate (and what for) when the salary is off the table…

Eight Benefits to Negotiate Other Than Salary

"Price doesn't make deals, and salary doesn't control your career."
Christopher Voss, businessman, author, professor and former FBI negotiator

You've snagged the job of your dreams, but there's just one problem. It doesn't come with a dream salary. Do you really have to walk away from it? Not necessarily, not if you can negotiate other benefits to make the overall package more palatable.

Salary typically accounts for 70% of an overall package, with benefits making up the remaining 30%, so their value is not inconsiderable.

We all know that salary is negotiable, but the truth is that a lot more can be as well. It may or not be expressly stated but certain non-salary benefits such as flexi-time, vacation allowance, titles and more can be up for negotiation as well.

The good news is that if your potential employer is as keen for you to work for them as you are, they may be prepared to find a little wiggle room elsewhere if they can't increase the salary. Indeed, some of these come at little to no cost to the company but can make a big difference to you.

Non-salary benefits can potentially influence your future career development, so they are definitely worth asking for in your starting contract. Likewise, just because a company has never offered x, y and z benefits before doesn't automatically mean they will be unavailable to you, so it's worth an ask.

You may also be able to negotiate for some of these if you've been at the company for a while and have proven yourself a valuable member of the team.

Note that this list doesn't include pension or retirement schemes, 401(k) matches or insurance perks as these are specific to region and country. Your company may also offer other benefits not on this list.

Non-salary benefits to negotiate for include:

<u>An Improved Title:</u> Consider your potential role carefully: does the title adequately reflect it? Does it sound dynamic and likely to help you when you search for another job in the future? If the answer to either of those is 'no', ask for a different title. Ditch 'secretary', for instance, for 'executive assistant', or suggest your own title.

If you've been at the company for a while and added value to the organization, you should keep an eye out for possible areas of advancement and make your case when they crop up. Make a good argument and, if you can, find a mentor or sponsor to help prepare and advocate for you (research shows that those with sponsors have more career success).

<u>Commuting costs:</u> The average employed Briton spends £146 a month (£305 a month in London) commuting to work. That's between £1,700 and £3,600 a year, give or take. Similarly, the average worker in the U.S. forks out $2,600 annually to do the same. If you're going to need to commute to work, and potentially clock up travel expenses while on work duties, tot up the expected amount and ask for a transport or mileage allowance or reimbursement. The

company may be willing to add this to your contract. Consider the potential benefit carefully as it can often make up for a lower salary.

Jason, an engineer now working for an international company in the UK, was a highly sought-after employee who had the good fortune to choose between two lucrative job offers. Both were in the same city with almost identical job roles and salaries, with very little to choose between them.

During salary negotiation, both companies managed to meet his target, one a little more generous than the other, but both indicated there was no money in the budget for more. He believed them but knew he should negotiate the rest of his benefits package as well. The company offering a little more salary offered a mileage allowance while the other offered the use of a company car, both a significant benefit since he lived outside the city and his job would involve significant travel.

Jason leaned towards the latter but made himself run the numbers to be sure. He discovered that as he was probably going to do more than 25,000 miles, a company car would be his most financially beneficial option and would make up for the slight salary shortfall. Plus, the company agreed to private use at the weekends. He took the job with the company car and hasn't regretted it since.

<u>Wardrobe Allowance:</u> Yes, this may only really be relevant if you're expected to meet high-level clients in your job (and jeans and a shirt just won't do), or alternatively if there's a uniform code to your job and you have to go out and buy relevant clothes before you start. If either of these applies, don't be afraid to petition for a stipend to cover it. Ask for it to be added to your contract.

<u>Extra Holiday or Vacation Time:</u> Your company may not be able to increase your base salary, but perhaps they could offer more vacation days. If you're negotiating a job offer, find out what the standard holiday allowance is and ask for double. Remember the key to negotiating… start high (but with a reasoned claim) and expect to go lower. Know what amount of vacation days would make the job palatable for you.

Currently, almost all workers in the UK are legally entitled to 5.6 week's paid holiday each year compared to the U.S.'s average 10 days of paid leave and six paid holidays per year.

If you're already working for a company, it may be worth asking for more holiday time at your annual review. You may find it easier to persuade the boss if you detail how you will minimize the impact of your absence (i.e., you will continue to check email and keep in touch with colleagues).

This may be more likely to be approved if you are a high-level worker or have proven yourself an asset to your firm. Likewise, if there is a special reason for the additional time off (honeymoon, family sickness).

Day-care fees: It can be almost prohibitively expensive to pay for day-care costs while going back to work, so ask the company what childcare options they have available. They may offer onsite child care, which you'll want to gain access to. If they don't offer anything specific, ask about getting a partial reimbursement on your childcare costs. After all, you don't want your entire salary or pay eaten up by it.

Flexitime/ Flexible Scheduling: This doesn't have to cost your company anything, but if your boss would allow you to work from home for one or two days a week, for instance, you would save on commuting charges and additional spending (buying lunch, for instance). This, plus a more relaxed schedule, could make up for a lower salary base. You could also negotiate your start and end times to fit around any children you need to collect from school etc…

Flextime is not as rare as you think, says research group Catalyst. They report four out of five graduates around the world work some sort of flexible working arrangement.

It's not just parents either. Half of all non-parent workers also cited flexible working as *'very or extremely important'*. Flex time includes job sharing, staggered starts and end times, reduced work schedules and shorter working weeks.

The key to negotiating flexi-time is to know exactly what you want and to ask for a specific schedule. It might be to leave early twice a week, working from home one day a week etc… Ask your HR manager if there is a policy in place to accommodate this, and if you make your case, demonstrate how you would still fulfill all your duties as effectively using flex time as you do now.

Suggest a trial period if people seem reluctant.

Note that under UK law, everyone including non-parents who have worked at their company for more than 26 weeks has a legal right to request flexible working once a year for whatever reason.

The employer must then legally consider it.

Shelley, 27, didn't want to return to her office-based administrative role five days a week after she had her first child but needed to continue working in some description once her maternity leave was over. *"I didn't quite know what I wanted, but ideally I wanted to work from home for two or three days a week. I just wasn't sure if it was possible since I worked as a personal executive assistant and I often needed to be in the office."*

Under UK law, however, her company had to consider her request, though not necessarily to approve it. Before submitting it, she spoke to a friend who was more senior than her in the company. *"I'm so glad that I did, as she taught me a lot about the internal politics of the company, especially everything I'd missed while out on maternity leave".*

"She convinced me that my application would be turned down if I asked for so much, and suggested alternatives instead. One alternative was to ask for staggered start and end times, plus one day working from home. That's the option I decided to go with."

In the end, the company decided they needed someone in the office full-time but offered another solution. The person covering Shelley's job during maternity leave was keen to stay on, so if Shelley wanted, they could job share. It meant fewer hours (Shelley was offered three days a week, albeit in the office, but there was the prospect of staggering the start times so she could come in a little later.) The other candidate would do two-and-a-half days (half-a-day to 'switch over'), and each would cover for the other's holidays.

"Yes, it meant less money, but I also had the option for some unrelated freelance work from home on my days off that wouldn't interfere with my contract, so I took it. Now I work three days a week and cover full-time for holidays or any impromptu absences. The company seems happy as they have better coverage, and I'm happy as I can spend two days at home with my baby. It's worth cutting back on some costs to do that." Shelley has since learned that if she hadn't asked for flexible working in the first place, a job share would never have been offered.

Guaranteed Severance: No-one likes to contemplate losing their job, especially before you've even started, but we no longer have jobs for life anymore. Tough times can even mean we might be out of a job in a year's time, and if that happens, you need to make sure you protect yourself. Ask for a guaranteed severance package should you lose your job through no fault of your own. Not only should this protect you and give you a bit of breathing room to search for a new job, but it may also make the company think twice about letting you go if they must pay you a generous severance package.

Reimbursement for Education and Tuition: Many companies are willing to pay employees to continue their education and training while working, recognizing that it is a direct investment back into the company. They may arrange to send you to conferences and seminars or even pay for your continuing education, so it's certainly a worthwhile request to make. Be aware of the small print here – some companies may limit professional development to your current area of work or may require you to work at the company for a certain number of years or else you pay back the tuition costs.

Relocation Expenses: If your company is asking you to move, you should be eligible for relocation expenses. Before you inquire about them, make sure you know how much would genuinely cover the costs of moving you and your family to another city. Removals firms often give free estimates, so it's worth asking for one before negotiating. Make sure too to check out the cost of renting or buying accommodation in your new area as it may be much higher than the area you currently live in.

Establishing Trust and Likability

In our last chapter, I talked about the importance of likeability, cited by Dr. Robert Cialdini, the 'Godfather of influence', as one of his six key principles of persuasion. Simply put, people are more likely to say yes, agree to terms and be influenced by people that they like. Research proves it, time and time again.

The natural extension of likability is trustworthiness.

Being likable and trustworthy helps to reduce the potential for conflict in negotiation. Remember, you don't need to be adversarial, hostile or an aggressive type A personality to win in a negotiation; charm will take you further than a snarl. (In the fable it was the gentle sun that made the man remove his coat and not the aggressive wind!)

In my last chapter, I gave you some pointers for establishing likability. Now I'm going to talk a little about establishing trust between you and your negotiation counterpart.

Building the Trust

"The best way to find out if you can trust somebody is to trust them."
Ernest Hemingway

Trust is integral to a negotiation. In fact, it's difficult (but not impossible – read on!) to negotiate without trust. If you don't believe a word the other person says, how can you have any confidence in their promises during a negotiation?

Trust usually develops naturally over time, but that's often a luxury that negotiators don't have. Many inexperienced negotiators, therefore, choose to play it safe instead, making cautious deals, giving few concessions and keeping their cards close to their chest (breaking one of Adam Grant's Best Practice suggestions for sharing information).

In contrast, experienced negotiators know how to foster trust on the fly, encouraging faith by establishing their own trustworthiness at the bargaining table. All of which leads to bigger and better deals and satisfied business partners (and bosses).

So, where to start?

<u>Look to Your Reputation</u>

"It takes 20 years to build a reputation and five minutes to ruin it."
Warren Buffett

Before you even get around the bargaining table and meet your negotiating counterpart, you can bet they've Googled and researched the heck out of you. And, hopefully, you've done the same to them. Your reputation, therefore, is the first sign of whether you are trustworthy or not, so don't neglect it.

Your reputation precedes you, and a bad one can kill a deal from the start. A solid impressive reputation, in contrast, can give the other side the confidence they may need to take a leap of faith on you if negotiations reach an impasse at any stage.

Consider your reputation a tool. (Don't forget, as per Dr. Cialdini's principles of persuasion, you want to establish yourself as an authority). So, include media and trade reports on your website, include references from mutually trusted third parties as to your credibility and other items demonstrating past successes.

Conversely, remove incriminating posts or photos on social media that portray you in a negative light. You don't need last weekend's drunken stag party photos of you downing a Yard of Ale and promptly throwing up, for instance, to be the first thing a potential customer sees when they Google you. It doesn't quite send the right professional message, though it may have been fun!

Speak their Language

Many businesses and professions have unique specialized jargon or terms, and if you want to demonstrate your qualifications as a trusted authority, you need to know and use them. If you demonstrate that you don't know the basics of the language a potential client uses while trying to gain their business, for instance, it will be near impossible for them to think of you as anything other than unprepared and therefore untrustworthy.

Take the time to learn, understand and appreciate the other party's history and culture, as well as language and perspective. You will send a clear message that you are committed to the relationship in the longer term and to the negotiation in front of you, a key step in building trust.

Of course, it doesn't mean that you won't make mistakes or gaffes now and again, especially if you're not familiar with your potential new client's profession. However, if you express your desire to understand the company's policies and ethos at the outset – and stress that you have already been working to do so – your negotiating counterpoint is more likely to think leniently towards you than otherwise.

I have had the great privilege of working with both editorial creative people in my career, and with the technical team behind them on the internet. Two separate sets of people, different backgrounds, abilities and skill sets, working together on one final product… which was a problem at times because the two sides often didn't know how to speak to one another.

The coders struggled to 'dumb down' their work to the creatives (without being patronizing), and the creatives didn't know the 'technical speak' to express their desires to the tech team. Meetings between the two were often long-winded and frustrating as both sides struggled to understand the other. We were all working on the same product and goal but there was always a huge pressure to produce and succeed for both teams. It meant that trust became an issue and far too many people played the blame game.

The breakthrough came in the form of two people – myself (I don't mean to sound bigheaded here, so bear with me) and a coder. We'll call him Damian. Damian was unusual in the tech team because he could speak plain English. I'm not being unkind to coders or programmers here, but it's often hard to explain your work to people who don't know your 'language'. I'm sure many of them would agree with me.

Damian, luckily, was a coder who understand creatives and who could also explain why so-and-so functionality didn't work or wasn't possible in ways that they would mostly understand. Or alternatively, he could explain it to me in a way that I understood, and I could 'translate' it for him when necessary. We made a good team.

My role in liaising with the tech team as a born and bred creative also helped. I had to work hard to understand their work, their pressures, ethos and terminology. It helped that I'm a geek at heart (don't tell anyone) and found it fascinating.

I could understand and talk to them and they knew I would listen to their concerns and try to find a way forward that kept both parties happy. It also helped that I took them out to the pub a few times as well (who doesn't like expenses-paid for drinks!).

Slowly, communication improved, both sides learned to trust one another, and negotiations became much more fruitful. Win-win!

<u>Smile and Be Competent</u>

Psychologists have discovered that people who portray themselves as 'warm' – friendly and non-competitive – make people feel they can trust them. If you seem competent, people are also more inclined to respect you, which enhances that trust further.

Demonstrating warmth is the most important first step, says Harvard psychologist Amy Cuddy. Competence can then come next. In Cuddy's book Presence, she says: *"From an evolutionary perspective, it is more crucial to our survival to know whether a person deserves our trust."*

Smiling is, of course, one way to make yourself more likable to people, and as we know, people prefer to do business with people they like.

Be Prepared to make Unilateral Concessions

"It takes two to do the trust tango--the one who risks (the trustor) and the one who is trustworthy (the trustee); each must play their role."
Charles H. Green, The Trusted Advisor

This strategy is particularly useful if you're looking for a long-term relationship with your negotiating counterpart. Offering a carefully crafted concession – ideally one that costs you little but offers genuine benefit to the other side – can do wonders for trust. Not only does it indicate that you understand what the other side deems important and valuable, but it also suggests to them that you are in this relationship for the long haul.

Negotiation in long-term relationships tends to include less of the tallying of wins and losses that dealing with strangers usually entails. It suggests that you see a future relationship between the two of you and that you are willing to take the first step to achieve it.

Of course, there's a caveat. If you are willing to make a concession during negotiations, unilateral or otherwise, you must make sure that the other side acknowledges it as such.

You'd be surprised how effectively people can discount or devalue concessions as not important or relevant, purely because they don't want the obligation of reciprocating. Cue resentment followed by hardball tactics.

The solution to this is to label your concession, to let the other side know what it is costing you to make it and what sacrifices you are making as a result. You will not only ensure they appreciate your concessions but demonstrate your goodwill, boost mutual trust and hopefully trigger the other side's willingness to reciprocate.

Let me issue a quick warning here before I move on: be authentic when you do this. Don't fall into the trap of walking into a meeting room with a set of fake 'needs' that you intend to bargain away, pretending to make major concessions when really you haven't made any at all. While this tactic can sometimes work, it's often obvious to the other side, especially if they've done their homework, and they won't appreciate the disingenuousness.

Explain Your Demands
It may seem obvious to you why you are asking for the demands that you are during a negotiation, but it's not necessarily so to the other party. In fact, the other party will often instinctually assume the worst about your intentions.

Research shows that while we view ourselves in the best possible light, we tend to view others less favorably, especially people we are in conflict with. So, if you cannot accept a particular deal on the table because of budget constraints or because the people you represent have given you strict instructions, explain that to the other party if you can. It may feel counterproductive, but it will increase trust.

Make your case for your demands, explain why you ask for certain things. A justified demand or offer will seem less extreme than one without any explanation or background and is more likely to preserve and even enhance trust.

If you must charge an extra commission for certain elements of a deal, for instance, perhaps because you use outside labor or agents in that particular arena, explain that to the client or the person you're negotiating with. True, it won't make their bottom line any less, but it should mean they can trust you more. If they can see you're not deliberately trying to rip them off, they may even agree to your demands.

How to Negotiate with Someone You Don't Trust

This chapter has been all about trust so far, but what happens if you don't or can't trust the person sitting across from you at the negotiating table? Is it still possible to negotiate in good faith?

This might be a controversial answer, but I say yes. IF you take some precautions.

The very first thing you should do is to check their credibility; there's nothing worse than to go through an excruciating negotiation only to discover that the person you've been talking to is not empowered to negotiate the agreement in the first place. Don't take their word for it – if you don't trust them, how can you assume they'll tell the truth? Even if they don't lie to you, they could be fooling themselves as to their importance. Instead, verify with someone else in their company or with a third-party that they can do what they say.

If they are not as empowered as they suggest, you have a choice: carry on with the meeting and use it to pick up as much information as you can before your real negotiations or cancel the meeting and seek one with someone who is empowered to make an agreement instead.

Assuming they are empowered to carry out the negotiation, how can you limit your risk? There's no doubt that negotiating with someone you don't trust changes the whole nature of the discussion. Whereas before you may have been ready to put your cards on the table, you cannot do that here simply because you have no idea how they will react.

As such, your best bet is to negotiate slowly and in smaller increments. Make slow moves and ensure 100% recorded agreement before moving on.

You'll find these steps helpful:
Control the note-taking process – ensure you are the one to make the notes (or have someone else on your team do it) and you agree to draw up the documents recapping any agreements. Include a name next to each agreed item, indicating who is responsible for it.

When you do draw up the final agreement, ensure you link your actions to the other party's. Sample wording, for instance, could be 'If you do this, I will…" This gives you leverage and helps to ensure that what is agreed actually gets done.

How to Deal with Brinkmanship
Imagine you have a deal to supply 100 electronic tablets to a business but the client rings to say he's reviewed the specs again and his company doesn't need half of the features available on them. As such, he will pay 10% less than agreed, or you can cancel the deal.

The problem is that the tablets are already on their way to the company. What do you do?

Refuse and the deal may collapse altogether, along with the expected maintenance contract of those tablets in the future. Agree, and you've just taken a financial hit through no fault of your own.

That is brinkmanship, my friend, and it's a hard nut to crack. It's a negotiation strategy designed to push you to agree to a set of extreme conditions or lose the deal entirely. Some people use brinkmanship to demonstrate strength and to let you know who holds the balance of power in the negotiation, but it's a high-risk strategy.

I'm sure you can imagine how detrimental it can be to goodwill, plus it threatens a complete breakdown in negotiation and business. Risky if the client is bluffing, in particular.

So, how can you defend yourself against brinkmanship and ensure you never get put in such a position?

First, know your vulnerabilities. If the other party's service or product is critical to your business, or you've made an irreversible commitment to the project with high switching costs, you are vulnerable to potential brinkmanship. Of course, we all hope the other party would prefer to make a long-term beneficial arrangement instead of resorting to such brute tactics, but it's worth taking steps to avoid such vulnerabilities anyway.

Protect yourself by diversifying your suppliers so no single supplier can hold you to ransom, avoid making irretrievable commitments until you have a signed commitment/ deal, and always present business as booming, suggesting you're not relying on this one deal for success (even if you are!).

Inform your client that the price of the deal may alter if he or she requires additional services, specs or functionalities, and be sure to review the price regularly. Inform the client of the new price as the scope increases; this makes it harder for them to renegotiate at the last minute if they've accepted everything so far.

If you do find yourself subject to brinkmanship despite the above, how should you react? You can call his bluff and see if he backs down (but be prepared to take your business elsewhere if he doesn't) or attempt to speak to someone more reasonable in the company. If you have no alternative but to accept his demands, try to consider it a strategic defeat for the sake of the company but make sure it can't happen again in the future.

Alternatively, attempt some form of a brinkmanship of your own. Perhaps you could offer to supply the tablets at the reduced price if you first remove all the functionality that he says he doesn't need. He may or may not blink first but beware that this is a high-risk tactic that could further damage your relationship with the company.

What to Do when Negotiation Fails

No matter how good a negotiator you are, you're going to experience some negotiation losses. No method guarantees success every time.

So, what should you do if a negotiation fails? Walk away? Here's where your **BATNA** – *Best Alternative to a Negotiated Agreement* – comes in.

Before you enter into any negotiation, you should be aware of what your BATNA is. If you're negotiating for a used car, for instance, because you need one before starting your new job, you should know what your independent alternatives are if you cannot come to an agreement over the particular used car of your choice.

In this case, your BATNA could include going to another used car dealer, investing more money and buying a new car from another dealer or using public transport to get to work.

Your BATNA should ideally satisfy or meet your major interests and you should consider all alternatives before rejecting them. Perhaps you considered buying a motorcycle instead, for instance, but rejected that idea because your work is quite a way away and you don't want to travel that far on a motorbike in potentially bad winter weather. You rejected a bicycle for the same reason.

Work to strengthen your BATNA before you meet your car dealer; perhaps you could test drive other cars, for instance, try out public transport options or discuss options with other car dealerships first so you can go in armed with a list of prices.

When negotiating for your ideal car, keep your alternatives in your back pocket. You are looking for success here and using your BATNA too early can be perceived as a threat.

Of course, if your negotiating counterpart assumes that you have no other option but to negotiate with them and try to take advantage as a result, you could educate them gently. Don't use it as a weapon but confess that you have your alternatives, as do they, and try to frame a potential deal between the two of you as being better than both of your respected BATNAs.

If you really cannot come to an agreement, or the other person tries to bully you with their BATNA, consider walking away and implementing your alternatives.

Now that we've cracked negotiation in a professional setting, let's move closer to home… our next chapter talks about negotiation with your nearest and dearest, family and friends in a personal setting. All of which can have ramifications just as important, if not more so, than your career success. So, read on!

Chapter Seven: Negotiating in your Personal Life

There comes a time (or many of them) when we need to negotiate in our personal lives, whether it's with a spouse, significant other, friend or our children.

Just this week, for instance, my husband and I disagreed on what to do with the garden (we live in a hot country and it's near on impossible to grow grass here), how often to have the air conditioning on in the bedroom (I like it cold, with a sheet; he prefers it slightly warmer without a sheet) and how to save for our children's potential university years.

Yes, I'm aware that the last one is a bit of a biggie. The first two issues I certainly have an opinion on (a nice seating area alongside a play area for the girls, give me the air conditioning remote already!).

But that last one needed a bit of delicate negotiation.

The options: save in a bank account and hope the exchange rate/ future economic uncertainty in the country doesn't whittle its value away or buy cheap land now and hope that it rises significantly in value in the future. I voted for the former, my hubby for the latter.

Of course, our girls are only three years old at the time of writing (soon to be four) so we have a few more years before it becomes an issue, but I like to know that we have a plan. I'm a planner, my hubby not so much. We know this about each other because we have run into this problem before.

So, we sat down and discussed/ negotiated our way through it. It took several chats, a lot of scribbling on paper, some irate responses, extra time needed to cool down, and some more chat.

And we came up with a solution… we're going to do both. Or at least, we're going to try to. So, we'll look for extra, extra, cheap land now with some of our savings, and then any spare money earned after that will go into an untouchable bank account for the girls. Job done, well apart from actually doing of the earning and saving part. Hopefully, that will come next.

I'm happy with the plan, and so is my husband. We both got a little of what we wanted. I'm glad that we're not putting all our money into one basket and are taking advantage of the 'safer' option (bank). Meanwhile, my husband is pleased that we're still going to invest and take a chance on higher returns from land, albeit by not spending as much initially.

It took a lot to get us to this point, but negotiation was the key. Coming as we do from two different countries, cultures and religions, we've come to respect the power of negotiation to keep us on track. While we agree about the bigger things – life ethos, family, commitment, hopes and dreams for the future – we often have differences of opinions on the smaller stuff, usually based on how we were raised and brought up.

Having children, for instance, highlighted our different approaches to childcare, often throwing up things we had never even thought (or talked) about before. Again, we agree on the bigger things – keep them healthy, safe and loved; invest in their future; education is key – but sometimes we disagree on the best way to achieve that.

Cry it out, versus not crying it out; when to go to pre-school (me: send them NOW! Hubby: Wait until they're four years old – thankfully, I won that negotiation); how many toys are too many; whether to let them drink one cup of weak tea a day (the way my husband was brought up; I was horrified at the thought).

We've had to learn how to negotiate both the small and bigger things to stop them from becoming much larger issues in our marriage than they needed to be. We've been together for 10 years so far (here's to the next decade!), so we must be doing something right.

Chances are there will be times in your relationship when you and your nearest and dearest will have different desires, goals and wishes. That's when negotiation and persuasion is crucial, to allow you to come to a compromise or an understanding, with ideally both of your needs met. The same is true for wider family relationships and even with friends. And trust me, once children come along, it all ends up being about negotiation and persuasion as they grow up.

'Eat your peas and we will go swimming… If you stop taking toys from your sister, she will want to play with you more… If we spend ten more minutes at the park, you must help mummy tidy up at home. Deal?'

Relationship Negotiation!

Here's the problem… negotiating with your significant other or family or children can be tough. Harder than negotiating professional successes with strangers sometimes. You wouldn't think so, but it is.

Why? Well, let's face it, there's often more at risk in a personal negotiation, isn't there? Entire marriages and relationships sometimes. All of which means there's a lot of emotions swirling around in there, which can be hard to control.

Plus, if we're not careful, we fall into the trap of thinking that love relationships shouldn't need negotiation in the first place, that romantic relationships shouldn't need work at all. Shouldn't it all be hearts, glitter, unicorns and eternal unison? We say, 'I love you' and it's immediately happy ever after?

Sorry to burst your bubble, but that's a total myth. All relationships take effort, communication and sometimes sheer hard work. So, it's worth taking the time to learn how to negotiate with those who matter the most.

<u>My Tips For Negotiating with a Partner</u>
<u>Listen</u>

Way back in chapter three, oh so very long ago, I talked about the power of listening. I'd like to echo that now, and stress that listening is probably the most important of all the negotiation tips I'm about to provide.

Remember, listening means genuinely hearing the other person, not just impatiently waiting for them to shut up so that you can have your turn.

Think of it this way – without properly listening to each other, how can you know what the other truly wants, feels and is upset by? Failing to listen to one another is a sure-fire road to argument avenue rather than negotiation neighborhood. (Yes, I know I flogged that alliteration to death).

Be aware that negotiation isn't the same as conversation, so try not to slip back into the latter. 'Check-in' instead. Take turns to say what is on your mind – a stream of consciousness if you like – while the other actively listens. When you've finished, say 'Check' to indicate the other person's turn. You must then listen to them, silently giving them all your attention.

The benefit of this is that you'll just say what's on your mind when it's your turn again, so you don't need to plan ahead or get distracted making a prior argument in your head.

'Checking in' may feel a little awkward at first if it's a communication style you're not accustomed to, but it's a useful technique to try.

<u>Remember you're on the Same Team</u>
It's all too easy to slip into an adversarial position when you enter negotiations, but in a personal relationship, that's a mistake. You may want different things right now – you don't want to cook every night, or you want a home-cooked meal every night – but communally, you want the same end goal. A happy relationship and food to nourish it and you.

As I said above, my husband and I may disagree about many of the smaller things, but we know we're working together to achieve the bigger, major ones (happy family, happy life etc…). Keeping that in mind at all times helps to avoid the adversarial and the competition that can sometimes arise between spouses when things aren't quite going the way you want them to.

Compromise doesn't have to be win or lose. If you keep in mind that you're working together to create something amazing; turn it into a win/ win by focusing on what you both gain instead of what you're losing.

Watch your Language
I'm not talking about swearing or foul language – though it's also a good idea to watch that when you're potentially angry too – but more the language that you choose when asking for help or trying to persuade someone.

In his book Men are from Mars, Women are from Venus, author John Gray, for instance, argues that women often use the 'wrong language' when asking men to do things.
Women, Gray says, ask things like 'Could you…?' which leaves the man with no opportunity to refuse because yes, it is physically possible to do whatever task she has asked.

But what if the man doesn't want to do it, or would prefer to do it later? That's when small resentments build, which can damage a relationship.

Instead, Gray argues, if women simply said, 'Would you?' instead, it opens up the opportunity for the man to say 'yes, but I'll do it in five minutes' or, 'I would but it sets off my asthma.'

Gray points out that even such a small change can make a big difference to a relationship, even after many years together.

I'm going to talk more about the power of language in chapter nine, persuasive language in particular. You'll want to make sure you read that chapter, it's a fascinating topic.

Talk Through Your Assumptions

While working together is important in a relationship to make sure you're heading in the same direction, knowing your own preferences is too. Make sure you're aware of what you desire versus what your partner desires.

Then, consider how your understanding of your partner's preferences influences your own. When you do this, demonstrate your work/ thinking in order to avoid making incorrect assumptions.

Jack and Trudy, for instance, live in Oxford in the UK. A few years ago, Jack, who works in the building trade, was contemplating a merger with another business. Jack was in favor of the move, but Trudy worried that Jack would lose his autonomy and if anything went wrong, their life savings.

Secretly, she also worried that it would take the couple back to their earlier years, when they were working all hours to establish their new business, hardly leaving any time for each other. As Trudy said of that time, "It nearly broke us. I wanted to be supportive of Jack and his dreams, but I hardly ever saw him and when I did, he was so stressed it wasn't pleasant."

Jack had been trying to persuade Trudy of the benefits of a merger for several weeks, and the couple had a lot of arguments and misunderstandings during that time. It was a frustrating period for both of them.

Finally, Jack threw his hands up. He told Trudy, "OK, if you don't want us to merge, we won't. I know you're worried about the money, so to stop you worrying, we'll stay as we are."

Jack admitted that he secretly hoped his magnanimous gesture would encourage Trudy to change her stance too (remember how we talked about reciprocation earlier). He confessed to being frustrated that she wouldn't support him and angry that she considered money more important than his well-being because his primary reason to merge was to stand down from the day to day running of the company and have more time for a family. Of course, Trudy didn't know any of this… because Jack hadn't told her.

She had assumed Jack's ambition drove the merger, while Jack had assumed Trudy primarily cared about the money. Neither assumption was correct.

Finally, Trudy responded to Jack's gesture with honesty. "I told him that while, yes, I was a little worried about the money, I was more concerned that he would throw himself back into the company and I would never see him again.

"I was 28 at the time, and I wanted children. It felt like time was passing us by. I wanted us to try now, but how could we if he had new business responsibilities?"

Of course, once Jack heard that, he told Trudy of his wish to step down to devote more time to their potential family too. He had kept that part of the plan to himself in case it didn't turn out to be possible in the short term; he didn't want to disappoint her.
The irony is that Jack and Trudy both wanted the same thing… and once they discussed it, Trudy could see how the merger could give them exactly what they wanted. With their new agreement in mind, the merger went ahead. Jack and Trudy went on to have three children and both cite the merger as one of the best things they ever did.

But imagine that conversation again if Jack hadn't mentioned the money. If he'd just said, "OK honey, I know you're worried about the merger, let's put it on hold or cancel it for now and talk about it in a few years' time."

Trudy may have taken him up on it without any further discussion. The result? Jack may have resented the decision, plus he wouldn't have had more time to devote to starting a family. Who knows how many children, if any, they would have had by now?

Make a point of stating your assumptions when it comes to your partners' preferences and you will give them the chance to correct your misunderstandings.

<u>Don't Assume Your Partner 'Owes You One'</u>
At some point in negotiation between spouses or significant others, there is usually give and take. Sometimes you'll give more than you take, but if that's the case, don't assume that your partner 'owes you one.'

If your partner doesn't share that assumption, he or she will be blindsided when you bring it up later, and you'll be resentful when he doesn't return a supposed favor. You can either give freely or expressly state your repayment options.

For instance, if you go out when you really want to stay in one night because your partner wants to try a new restaurant, you could always ask that repayment include a night in the following night, or a night out to the restaurant of your choice the following week. Don't keep a silent tally as it will only foster resentment.

A Quick Word about Negotiating with Friends

Before we come to talk about one of the most perilous negotiation tasks you can face – negotiating with the kids – let's talk briefly about discussions and persuasion between friends.

Imagine the sort of decisions you make between friends… anything from when to meet up, where to eat out, what wine to choose, where to vacation together or what joint birthday presents to buy, to whether your friend will be Godmother/ father to your child, when to arrange a class reunion or how best to support your friend in an emotional time of need or crisis.

And that's just the tip of the iceberg, or whatever your favorite lettuce happens to be.

The good news is that friends appear to achieve better negotiated outcomes than strangers and even romantic partners, says research from Stanford and Cornell University.

Researchers Margaret Neale, Kathleen McGinn and Elizabeth Mannix examined negotiation role-play between friends, strangers and life partners and concluded that a *"curvilinear relationship"* exists tying together how close negotiating partners are and the gains they can expect to achieve from negotiations.
Simply put, negotiating friends and couples have an added advantage over strangers when it comes to negotiations, primarily because they know each other's preferences.

Friends, however, typically tend to do even better than couples because the latter are often averse to conflict. It's also likely that couples prefer to look for Symbolic Outcomes – the message they send to each other through their actions in a negotiation. If a husband foregoes the movie he wants to see in favor of his wife's preference, for instance, he sends her a message that he will sometimes place her wishes above his. Such reciprocal concessions can encourage positive reactions in the future.

There is one danger when friends or a group negotiate, however, and that is that you may end up going to Abilene…

The Abilene Paradox

For those of you who don't know, Abilene is a town in Texas with a nickname of the 'Friendly Frontier'. Despite its attempts to appear welcoming, however, it has unfortunately been linked with a fable demonstrating how no-one wants to go there.

That's a little unfair on Abilene, so let me explain.

The fable goes that on a hot afternoon, a family in Texas is playing dominoes on the porch when the father-in-law suggests driving miles north to Abilene for dinner. Everyone in the group slowly agrees. The wife says, ' great idea' while her husband, who secretly worries about the long hot drive, thinks he must be out-of-step so says it 'sounds good to me'. The mother-in-law also agrees on what a good idea it is.

True to fears, the drive is hot, long and dusty and the food poor once they do arrive. Four hours later, they arrive back home, exhausted, where each of them finally confesses that they didn't really want to go in the first place. Each one said yes to keep the others happy, and the father-in-law only suggested it in the first place because he thought everyone was bored.

Turns out they weren't bored, but they did each agree to take a trip that none of them wanted. Perplexing, huh?

This can happen easily with friends and family, who often want to keep each other happy, but it can also occur in professional negotiations and businesses too, where no-one contests decisions taken by a group because they believe it to be the consensus of all. In reality, however, none of the group agrees with the decision. An example would be a new way of working floated by the boss that everyone agrees with, at least in public. In private, team members heartily disagree, but because no-one expresses it, the new way of working is introduced. People then typically regret not speaking up in time.

You may wonder how on earth this situation, named as the Abilene Paradox by Jerry Harvey of George Washington University, can occur, but it's actually remarkably easy for it to happen in a professional setting as well as a friends' one.

For instance, people tend to go with the herd, they fear to be socially unacceptable or of breaking traditions. At work, we may be apprehensive to voice our concerns for fear of rocking the boat; leadership may be lacking, or there is little interaction (and honest discussion) between team members.

At home, we may be reluctant to break with a tradition that no longer serves us well but which we daren't admit. Sometimes we simply lack the capacity or don't have the information we need to judge the pros and cons of the suggestion.

I'm sure the real Abilene is a nice place – more than 100,000 people live there after all – but be prepared to speak up if you don't want to end up there.

Negotiating with Children

Oh my, here we come to the really hard part, negotiating with your own kids! Whole books have been written on this very subject, so I can only hope to scrape the surface within this chapter, but let's take a quick look at it anyway.

Rather than trying to rewrite War and Peace, let's narrow our focus a little and see how we can create win-win situations with our children.

Creating Win-Win Negotiations
I should point out that win-win situations aren't just for parenting or family situations. They're a good habit to try to get into, in any negotiation where you value the relationship between you and the other party. Of course, they are arguably of particular importance between spouses, partners, parents and children, where the ongoing relationship should be more important than any particular negotiation.

It might be easier to describe win-win negotiations as the opposite to win-lose negotiations or, as it effectively is, haggling. Here each party if trying to get the best result for themselves and do not care about the relationship between them. It's possible for both parties to be happy with the eventual resolution, but it is less likely. Even if they do reach an agreement, one party may suspect he or she has been defeated in some way.

In contrast, a win-win situation is one where you both work together to identify a constructive solution to the problem, one in which both of you are genuinely happy with the outcome. It requires effort from both parties and a willingness to listen to what really matters to the other person. It isn't always easy.

In our last chapter, I told you the story of our flexible worker Shelley. Shelley didn't want to return to her job full-time after her maternity leave and requested staggered start and end times, and a day working from home as an alternative.

That didn't work for her boss, who refused the request because he needed someone in the office five days a week. That could have been the end of the situation, and Shelley would have had a hard choice to make… resign or unhappily work full-time again.

Thankfully, the company valued Shelley and looked for a win-win situation. Together with Shelley, who had to agree, they came up with an alternate plan… a job share with three days a week in the office, staggered starts and additional holiday cover provision.

Why was it a win-win? Shelley was happy because she kept a job she loved but also had more time at home to devote to her child. The company was happy because they retained Shelley's expert services plus her maternity cover staffer, who they also liked, and boosted their coverage during holidays. I also suspect Shelley's maternity cover was a cheaper hire, so the company got five-and-a-half days cover for the price of five or less. Working together, they created a plan that worked for both of them.

Now let's see if we can learn how to do the same with children.

How to Create Win-Win Situations with Children
You may think that it's easier to tell children what to do rather than negotiate with them but trying to create win-win situations is one way to boost a child's self-respect and self-esteem.

As parents, we inevitably set boundaries and attempt to instill our morals and values to our children. But the very simple act of listening to your children – whether they win, lose or draw in a negotiation – can make them feel that they have a voice and therefore value.

Laura Markham, Ph.D. and author of Peaceful Parent, Happy Kids: How To Stop Yelling and Start Connecting, shares the following advice on creating win-win situations between parent and child.
First up, she stresses that some limits are firm and are NOT open to negotiation, so make that clear.
'Yes, you WILL wear clothes to school.'
'No, you do not bite when you're feeling angry'.
But sometimes, we can permit some choice.
'Do you want to wash your hands yourself, or do you want me to wash them?'
'Do you want to wear the pink shoes or the yellow ones?' (Always the pink ones in our house).
Of course, sometimes a limit is non-negotiable, but our child will try anyway. It helps to have a sense of humor here – and some wine chilling in the fridge for when you've finally got them to bed.

But being firm doesn't mean you have to be harsh.

'I know it's hard to stop playing and get ready for bed when your sister gets to stay up later. But when you're nine, you will too. Right now, it's time for bed. Let's go!'
(Having twins like I do means this isn't really a line that you can use!)
Sometimes, however, it's worth realizing that a little negotiation can go a long way. Look for solutions together, include your child and you'll be teaching them to look for win/win solutions in life. A good habit to get into.

'You want to stay at the park, but I need to go home and make the dinner. What can we do? How about we stay for another ten minutes and you help me tidy up when we get home? Sound good? Great, that works for both of us. Ten more minutes at the park… go!'

Whining or threatening, of course, (them not you) shouldn't win the day, but good arguments can. This sets them up for success in life.

I've been working on creating win-win situations with my girls, too. It doesn't always succeed, it can be frustrating, but the alternative can be even harder to manage.

One of the most embarrassing situations I experienced with my twins was when I took them to a bouncy castle. It should have been an easy trip, you would think, anyway. Hah. They had other ideas. They were in the midst of the terrible twos, and it was the very first time we went out without the stroller. (The stroller had become an important safety requirement due to their uncanny ability to run in opposite directions – very fast – at the exact same time).

But what could go wrong at the bouncy castle, I thought! Fool. Alone, I watched as they played happily on the bouncy castle, lulled into a false sense of security until their time was up. Oh dear, that's when it all went wrong.

Both refused to come off the castle, so I did the only thing I could; I paid for extra time (I know, coward) but when that finished too, I physically climbed into the castle myself to grab them (while being shouted at by the man in charge who told me I weighed too much, thanks mate).

I grabbed twin A first, my supposed lesser of two evils, but no-one had told her that, and she screamed, kicked and punched the air in massive tantrum mode. She flat out refused to put on her shoes. When I went back into the castle for twin B, twin A tried to run away (and there was nothing and no-one to stop her. No stroller as a backup to strap her into you see!).

I'd like to say that my order to stay halted her progress, but she was in full demonic child mode by then, so I had to forego twin B to grab twin A. Now I had a dilemma. I sat twin A down and luckily grabbed twin B as she came around for her lap of honor on the castle.

Ditto the screaming, crying and refusing to wear shoes. I was endeavoring to put them on (we had a ten-minute walk after this), when twin A decides to stand up on her chair, tips it over backward and bangs her head on the floor. Hard.

Jeez, Louise. Now her crying is real, twin B is still screaming, no-one has any shoes on, I have no-one to help me, a couple of people are watching and smirking (but not helping), and I want to cry. Isn't it uncanny how easily children can turn a professional, strong accomplished woman into a blithering mess?

I'd like to pretend I was in control of the situation but what can I say? Twins! Double the love but double the trouble! Two of them, only one of me. And other twin-related clichés and excuses. I honestly didn't know how I was going to get us home as they were both too heavy by now to carry, and I didn't fancy carrying one and practically dragging the other along the road.

So, I did the only thing I could think of… I called their father, who was working nearby and begged for help. After he stopped laughing, he told me he couldn't come just yet but would try to be there in 15 minutes.

Well, I couldn't face another 15 minutes of screaming in public, nor could I put them back on the castle because not only would they get their way, but if hubby couldn't make it (very likely), I'd have to do *this* all over again.

In desperation, I negotiated. I spotted a toy car ride (thankfully two of them side by side!) and told them they could have one ride if they put their shoes on before we went home.

Thankfully the lure of the red and yellow cars was enough to encourage them to stop crying and give it a go. Phew. Crisis narrowly averted.

In case you were wondering, daddy did actually turn up in five minutes – no doubt freaked by the panic in my voice – and found the girls happily riding the toy cars. He then walked us home and that was that.

Not my finest moment, mummy moments granted, but a small sample of negotiation. Now that they're a little older, I try to encourage the sort of win-win situations suggested by Laura Markham above. But it's definitely a work in progress. On that note, I still have more than my fair share of embarrassing parenting stories to tell and you'll probably learn a few more tales before this book is done. Lucky you.

Coming up in our next chapter, body language and 'mind reading'… it promises to be a fascinating chapter so read on!

Chapter Eight: Effective Body Language in Negotiation

"What you do speaks so loud that I cannot hear what you say"
Ralph Waldo Emerson

Here's a somewhat scary thought.... more than half of our communication with others and our subsequent impact in negotiations has nothing to do with the words we use. We choose our words so carefully, don't we, and yet we rarely think about the real unspoken language of business negotiation… our body language.

The reality is that the way we unconsciously use our body (and tone of voice) to communicate says much more than our mere words ever could. Non-verbal communication includes everything from facial expressions, posture and gestures, to the tone of voice, speech rate and more… and it's highly revealing.

An experiment in the late '60s and early 1970s attempted to demonstrate just how important body language is. Albert Mehrabian, currently Professor Emeritus of Psychology, UCLA, came up with the ***7-38-55 rule***. He postulated that body language accounts for 55% of our communication, the tone of voice 38%, while words alone account for a mere 7%.

Mehrabian has since complained of being misquoted, pointing out that his calculation only applied to one particular instance of communication, and that the exact figures would differ in different situations. He does still stress, however, that body language accounts for the majority of our communication.

It's not surprising when you consider exactly how much flexibility body language offers.
Italian-American linguist Mario Pei, for instance, estimated that humans produce up to 700,000 different signs, while scientists have identified that we use 21 different facial expressions to communicate

meaning. There are also thought to be more than 1,000 different postures and accompanying gestures.

"I speak two languages, Body and English".
Mae West

Learning about body language can transform your negotiations.

Janine Driver, the founder of the Body Language Institute, says: *"Body language is critically important. Probably at least 50 percent of the impact we make negotiating is done through body language, maybe more."*

Understanding and recognizing what your negotiating counterpart's gestures, facial expressions, postures and tonality means, can give you a heads up in your next negotiation. It's the next best thing to reading their minds, which we all know is impossible anyway.

Recognizing body language cues can help make sure you're sending the right message, plus help you to recognize if your negotiation is going off-track, or if you've lost a person's interest. God forbid, you encounter a liar but it can also help you to detect one or someone you shouldn't trust in a negotiation.

There's a reason Driver, a body language expert, best-selling author and former federal law enforcement officer, is known as 'lyin tamer' -- she can detect dishonesty a mile away, thanks to a person's body language.
However, let's start first by looking at how you can send the right message through your own body language…

How to Send the Right Message
Most of our body language is unconscious and can give us away in an instant. But if you can learn to control and hone it, it can be one of your strongest assets in a negotiation.

As Driver says: *"You can have great talking points and a good pitch, but what people will really care about is whether they like you. The bottom line is we want to give good deals to people we like."*

The good news is that there are various nonverbal measures you can take to psychologically win favor with others.

Look Confident

Studies have shown that people who appear confident or even overconfident achieve a higher status than their less confident counterparts. One such study states that 'overconfidence leads to a behavioral signature that makes the individual appear competent to others'.

Confident people tend to be more admired, listened to, wield more influence and achieve more as a result. The good news is that you can use body language to fake confidence until you make it.
"As you act, so you become," says body language expert Lillian Glass, author of **The Body Language Advantage**. She shares some of her tips for demonstrating confidence through body language, the first being to keep your chin up at all times.

Glass says: *"Confident people are always looking up, never down at the table, the ground, or their feet. You have to always pretend that there's a string holding the crown of your head up."* Good posture and standing up straight goes along with that; slouching only serves to make you look disinterested and unprofessional.

Body language experts also recommend keeping your feet in an open stance about a foot apart pointing outwards, rather than together, as the latter indicates timidity. *"A confident person literally has two feet firmly planted on the ground,"* says Glass.

If you're a fan of Grey's Anatomy, think of Dr. Amelia Shepherd and her pre-op routine. To make herself feel strong and confident, she stands legs wide apart, hands on hips, body straight, head held high… all designed to give her confidence as she goes into surgery. She may be fictional, but she has a good point.

Making eye contact is, of course, essential and, says Glass, is probably the biggest indicator of confidence there is. She shares a trick to making effective eye contact if it's something you struggle with.

Start by looking into someone's eyes for two seconds, then look at their nose for two seconds, then their mouth for two seconds and then their face as a whole for two seconds. Do this on rotation and the other person shouldn't be able to tell that you're not looking into their eyes the whole time.

Other body language tips to demonstrate confidence include:

Don't Put Your Hands in your Pockets: We hide our hands when we're nervous, so avoid putting them in your pocket as it suggests you're uncomfortable.

Develop a firm handshake: It may sound simple, but experts say that strong confident people have a firm handshake, while weak people have a weaker offering. So, go for a strong handshake, with the palm facing slightly downwards.

Cut out words such as 'like' and 'um': people judge confidence by the way you speak.

Focus on others: Demonstrating an interest in others is a sure-fire way to portray confidence and has the added benefit of ensuring you're not focused on what they think of you. Says Glass: *"The bottom line is be interested, not interesting. Be more focused on the other person and what message is being communicated than focused on yourself and your self-consciousness."*

There are other things you can do to make sure you send the right message with your body language too, all of which will help to boost your power in a negotiation. They include:

Strategic Seating
Even the seat you choose at the negotiation table can potentially impact the results of the negotiation, and if you're not careful, can create a feeling of unconscious confrontation. Which is why Janine Driver, of the Body Language Institute, warns: *"Do NOT sit directly*

opposite the person you are trying to persuade. That increases anxiety and makes the negotiation confrontational."

The ideal position to sit if you get the opportunity is a 30 to 45-degree angle away from them; the easiest way to do this is to adjust your body to such an angle when addressing others.

Be In the Middle
Here's a quick tip for you – if you're giving a presentation or taking group photos, try to place yourself in the middle. Those people standing in the center are psychologically perceived as being the most important.

"Use non-verbal communication to SOFTEN the hard-line position of others:
S = Smile O = Open Posture F = Forward Lean T = Touch E = Eye Contact N = Nod" – **Quote by Unknown Author**

Match Their Body Movements
You may have heard of a subtle technique called matching and mirroring, which can be a tremendously helpful body language tool for gaining unconscious favor with someone.

As I've already reiterated (several times) in this book, people prefer to do business with people they like. Let me take that a step further, and stress that people like to do business with people who are like them.

But how do you convince someone, especially a stranger, that you are 'like them' if they don't know you already? By matching and mirroring, that's how – essentially the art of copying their unconscious mannerisms, moves, body language and even repeating their words back to gain their trust.

So, if they cross their arms, for instance, you cross yours a few seconds later. If they lean back, so do you, ideally with a few seconds' time-lag. If they speak with their hands, so do you. You get the idea.

Why does this work? I remind you of my words above again: people like people who are like them. When someone copies our unconscious movements, we notice the resemblance on a subconscious level and believe they are similar to us. We get on with them better. The more we believe someone is 'on our wavelength', the easier it is to develop a rapport and trust at an unconscious level.

Have you ever watched two best friends who are really in tune with one another? As well as sharing the same ideals, they often share the same mannerisms, without even realizing it. One might push her hands through her hair and the other unconsciously copies it, seconds later. Or they might share a similar laugh or smile.

As psychologist Barbara Fredrickson, the Kenan Distinguished Professor of Psychology at the University of North Carolina says, we mirror each other when we feel a connection. That backs up a Duke University study which demonstrates that physically doing what other people do helps them to feel comfortable.

This is called developing rapport (the desired end goal of matching and mirroring) and some charismatic people can do this instinctively. For the rest of us, however, the good news is that it is something that can be learned and a skill that we can cultivate throughout our lives, in all of our relationships.

How to Develop Rapport

First, decide who you want to emulate. It could be the person you're directly negotiating with, or another person – an influencer – in the room. Driver offers the following clue to identifying who that may be: she says if all the belly buttons at a meeting table are pointing towards one person, that's the influencer who you want to emulate.

She recommends subtly imitating the influencer three or four seconds after their body language, essentially 'mirroring' their trademark moves. *"If they lean back, you lean back,"* she says, reminding us that in order for the strategy to work, there must be a slight delay between the influencer's moves and your own.

A word of warning before we look at the sort of things you could copy: this needs to be subtle. The whole point is that it should generate an unconscious feeling of trust. If it's too obvious, it will make your intended 'target' uncomfortable.

If you're new to matching and mirroring, I would practice it on less important meetings and relationships first. I would also recommend focusing only on the unconscious elements of someone's behavior, such as tonality and physiology. According to our body language statistics above, these account for up to 93% of all communication anyway.

I saw a great picture recently that summed up rapport. David Cameron and Barack Obama, then the respective leaders of their countries, were walking in a field, suited and booted, with their suit jackets thrown over opposite shoulder, both smiling, giving the impression that they were completely in-sync and informal with one another. Now, I'm pretty sure both of these men know about matching and mirroring and adopt it frequently, but it still presented a powerful message of unity, probably exactly as they intended.

In your case, your negotiating counterpart may not be aware of the technique, so if you're subtle, it could work for you without the other person ever knowing why.

Communication Cues to Match

<u>Physiology:</u> Body language is so expansive, there are many different areas that you could match. Consider posture (slouching, standing, sitting, relaxed); facial expressions (brow furrowed or smooth, jaw tense or not etc…) and gestures (gesturing with hands in a particular way, tilting the head).

Tonality: When it comes to tonality – the tone of voice, volume, rate of speech – you need to be careful. While trying to match elements on tonality can be effective, it needs to be subtle. Don't start speaking in a high or completely different voice to match your client's, for instance. Instead, if your client speaks in a higher register than you, perhaps raise your voice just a little to match.

If they speak slower and more deliberately than you do, take care to slow your pace to one that is natural, subtle and more appropriate to theirs. Speaking at rapid-fire to someone who needs time to process is going to break rapport and lose the connection you have. If the opposite is true, consider speeding up just a little to reflect their pace. At all times, however, be yourself.

A Final Warning…
Matching and mirroring can be very effective when done well but be sure to use your common sense. Don't mimic every move a person makes; not only will it make your efforts more obvious, it's disingenuous. Likewise, do not copy negative body language or movements.

You want to seek rapport from a state of positivity; this is a technique intended to encourage a natural connection, not to fool them into believing you are someone you are not. Treat them with respect and dignity, and you should enhance your communication and subsequent relationship.

How to Read Other People's Body Language

Wouldn't it be great if there was a way to detect if someone was potentially open to negotiation before they even opened their mouth? If you could tell whether your pitch was winning or losing their interest without having to wait for their feedback? If this prior 'alert' gave you the chance to hone your negotiation on the go, and tailor it to the things that really mattered to them? If this knowledge could boost the chances of your success?

You can probably guess what I'm going to say now… Well, there is! Ta-da!

If you can read the non-verbal signs coming from your negotiating counterparts, you can significantly improve your negotiation successes. Their body language can tell you if they're interested in your pitch or are closed off and unlikely to reach an agreement. It can also help you detect deception.

Reading the Signs
Non-verbal indications that they are interested in your pitch include:

Leaning forward: the quintessential sign for wanting to know more

Opening their arms or legs: an invitation for further discussion

Going up on their toes: people tend to do this when enthused. Might be an idea to invest in a glass table so that you can see their feet!

Tilting their head: shows they are really paying attention, but you will need to assess whether they are demonstrating mere curiosity, or uncertainty.

A furrowed brow: also demonstrates concentration, as does the ability to ignore outside distractions.

Non-verbal clues that you are losing them include:

"Eye rolling is one of the nonverbal signs that is pretty much always aggressive"
Steve Watts

Pointing their feet away from you: again, you'll benefit from a glass table, but as a general rule, people tend to point their feet in the direction that they want to go to. So, if someone has their feet pointed towards the exit sign, it's a clue that they're not giving you their full attention.

Leaning back: opposite to the interest shown when leaning forward, people who lean back are trying to withdraw.

Crossing their arms: indicates a rejection of what you are saying.

Ditto crossed legs: crossed legs are a sign of low receptivity, and a bad sign, say, Gerard I. Nierenberg and Henry H. Calero, authors of How to Read a Person Like a Book. Out of 2,000 videotaped negotiations, not a single one was settled if a negotiator had their legs crossed.

Psychologist Travis Bradberry, Co-author of Emotional Intelligence 2.0, says in Entrepreneur: *"Psychologically, crossed legs signal that a person is mentally, emotionally, and physically closed off. It's not intentional, which is why it's so revealing."* Making them that much less likely to move in a negotiation.

Their smile doesn't reach their eyes: people often smile to hide what they're really thinking, so look at their eyes. A genuine smile crinkles the skin around the eyes, creating crow's feet.

How to Detect Deception

No-one likes to think someone may deliberately lie in a good-faith negotiation, but we've all been around the block enough to know that it happens. (Think back to our 'How to negotiate with someone you don't trust' section earlier).

"When the eyes say one thing, and the tongue another, a practiced man relies on the language of the first"
Ralph Waldo Emerson

Whether you can detect it or not, that's the real talent. People trying to deceive typically:

<u>Make too much eye contact:</u> we're always told to look people in the eyes and believe it's a sign of honesty, and it is… to an extent. What is lesser well known is that deceptive people will deliberately hold eye contact to try to cover up the fact that they're lying, often overcompensating and holding it for too long, making the other person feel uncomfortable.

But what's normal eye contact, and what's not? According to Travis Bradbury, Americans typically hold eye contact for seven to ten seconds, longer when we're listening than talking. Anything more, and they could be lying to you.

<u>Janine Driver warns of her 'top two tells' which are smirks and shrugs:</u> a smirk usually indicates some faking moral superiority, she says, and is a strong clue that someone is being misleading. A shrug indicates uncertainty, so if they are saying 'yes' but shrugging, they are keeping something secret.

<u>Movement that isn't integrated:</u> by this, I mean someone who waves their arms about excitedly, but their lower body remains stock still, or someone whose expressions stop at their mouth and not their whole face. Both examples indicate they are faking it.

Who knew that you could say so much without words?!

Hopefully, I've given you plenty to think about in this chapter, and we're not quite finished yet. Read on for our next and final chapter, the fascinating art of persuasive language…

Chapter Nine: Persuasive Language: Getting People to Yes in Negotiation

"Persuasion is often more effectual than force."
Aesop

'Sticks and Stones May Break My Bones but Words Can Never Hurt Me'
That's what we tell children, isn't it, as we try to make them feel better about bullying or name-calling? If only it were true! Words can most definitely hurt us, sometimes irrevocably so. Granted, it's not the only fib we tell kids – Father Christmas, the Easter Bunny, Tooth Fairy, 'you played a great game', 'it's chicken'… take your pick.

But if we didn't know just how much words could hurt us, we'd never need to pretend that they don't. You see, words have great power, and for our purposes, some have persuasive power in particular. Certain words and phrases, for instance, carry an inbuilt persuasive influence that you've probably never even thought about, let alone learned how to use.

That's a missed opportunity that we're going to correct right now.

It is my hope that this chapter triggers an interest in persuasive language patterns that you can follow up with further reading.

I know, I know, you're probably thinking back to our last chapter on body language and wondering why you need to bother with words if they only account for 7% of communication. (If you weren't thinking that, feel free to skip right on past this paragraph).

Let me put it this way, if you were negotiating a big deal that could potentially secure your business's future for the foreseeable, wouldn't you want access to all the ammunition you could muster? Wouldn't your staff, whose jobs and livelihoods depend on the agreements you make, expect you to use every available asset at your disposal?

Yes, they would, and I'm sure you would too. Besides, when that 7% of communication is ultra-persuasive, it gains more force and brings even more benefits.

So, let me answer your next question: How can language be so persuasive and yet we're hardly aware of it?

The Power of Assumption
Think of language like a roadmap. A roadmap helps us find where to go, but it doesn't tell us everything, does it? It can't. In order to give us the key info, it deletes unnecessary information, distorts terrain and generalizes signs, colors and more to make it easier to understand.

We do the same sort of thing with language. We leave things out, make assumptions and generalize all the time in order to share information. We call these presuppositions. You may also hear them referred to as Hypnotic Language Patterns, which should give you some indication of how powerful they are.

What are Presuppositions?
Presuppositions are probably THE most persuasive language pattern there is, and, despite the convoluted name, are probably the simplest things to use too. You might already even use them without realizing as they are deeply embedded in our communication.

Let me try to explain. When we speak or write, both communicator and listener make multiple inbuilt assumptions – such as assuming at least part of a statement the other person has made is true in order to comprehend it. It's a natural predisposition. Otherwise, we would go around questioning everything that we hear, and we'd never get anything done.

If I told you a woman called Susan was leaving her home to drive to work, for instance, you would, of course, naturally assume there is a woman called Susan, she has a car and a home and a job. Why would you think otherwise? You assume it's true.

Likewise, if someone told you their car is blue, you automatically assume that, yes, they do have a car because they have told us they do. Instead, you focus on the color blue.

Here's another one. Let's stick with the car theme. If I told you that my neighbor John has bought a new car which is painted a horrible orange color, you would assume:

That John exists; He is my neighbor; He has just bought a new car; I have seen the new car; It's painted a horrible orange color.

You might also assume that I don't like said horrible orange color, and that John has little taste!

As German sociologist Georg Simmel says, *"Life rests upon a thousand presuppositions which the individual can never trace back to their origins and verify, but which he must accept upon faith and belief"*.

A lot of our presuppositions are shared and culture-related, good or bad.

Here's a great example of our instinctive use of assumption. If you've already heard this story, then this won't work on you, but if you haven't, see if you can answer the question…

There is a head-on collision on a motorway and both father and son are critically wounded. In the hospital, a surgeon works on the son for hours, desperately trying to save him. He dies on the table. When an assistant asks the surgeon to look at the other victim, the surgeon says, *"I couldn't bear it. I have just lost my son."*
Who is the doctor?
[SPOILER WARNING – don't read on until you've given your answer]

So, who is the doctor?

If you are anything like my husband, you're probably trying to work out how the father, critically injured, was well enough to work on the son. I confess I tried to give a pretty convoluted explanation of it too the first time I heard this. You will keep coming up against the same snag, however – the father is also dying, so how could he work on the son?

Of course, once you see the truth, you'll be a little shamefaced at your assumption. You see, most people assume the surgeon is male when in reality, it's the mother who operated on her son. See how inbuilt our presuppositions are?

"Most people catch their presuppositions from their family and surrounding society, the way that a child catches the measles," says Francis A. Schaeffer, author of **How Should We Then Live? The Rise and Decline of Western Thought and Culture.** *"But people with understanding realize that their presuppositions should be *chosen* after a careful consideration of which worldview is true."* Schaeffer's quote above reminds us of something: if we learn about presuppositions, if we're conscious of them, we can choose to use them to our advantage. How?

We can use them to persuade people to do what we want, in a nice way, of course.

I should point out here before you worry that I'm getting Machiavellian on you, that one or two presuppositions alone will not make someone do something that is against the moral core of their nature. Likewise, if you assume the use of a presupposition that blatantly isn't true (accuse someone of doing something they didn't do, for instance), the sharp juxtaposition will bring them out of the 'trance', as it were.

Using presupposition gently and with no intended malice can, however, lay the groundwork and subtly encourage someone into doing something they might want to do anyway. Think of it as giving you a head start in negotiations.

Why Do Presuppositions Work So Well?

"The tongue can paint what the eye can't see."
Chinese Proverb

Presuppositions can help people to 'see things your way'. How? Think of the assumption behind a presupposition as a dart. Assumptions bypass the conscious mind because we don't actively need to think about them and shoot straight into the unconscious instead. Once that happens, it is considered fact and bam! Your client or negotiating counterpart has just accepted the premise of your negotiation, without even realizing it. You have bypassed any resistance from your listener.

Types of Presuppositions
There are many different types of presupposition, such as:

Clauses of time: use the following words in your sentences and you extend the power of presuppositions. Time-related words such as: Before, During, While, After, When, End, Continue (and many more) can be used to make your presuppositions even more powerful.

Examples include:
"Would you like a coffee while you wait?" – we assume that you will wait.
"After you buy this book, you will know everything there is about (insert subject here) – yes, I've assumed you will buy the book.
"Before you go to the shop, I will take a shower" – heads up, you're going to the shops!
 There's a reason such clauses of time are used in traditional hypnosis: they work. Think of phrases such as, "While you listen to my voice, your eyes will start to feel heavy."

Awareness presuppositions: with these, you deliberately draw attention to one element of your statement, presupposing the rest. You'll use classic 'awareness' words such as:
Know, Aware, Realise, Notice, Understand, Remember, Discover, Wonder

These are classic words used in sales copy because they are so powerful. With these, you get people concentrating on how aware they are of the presupposition you're making, rather than the presupposition itself.

For instance, 'Do you realize you could drastically improve the health of your wallet in just two weeks?' The listener now assumes they really could be making money in just two weeks and is focused on how aware they are of it. That's when you then seal the deal and sell them your product.

"The secret is to always let the other man have your way."
Claiborne Pell

Techniques to Use When Using Presuppositions
The Double Bind: here you give the listener two choices, but here's the key – each one leads to the outcome you want.

"Do you want to tidy your room now or after dinner?"
The child can decide when to clean their room but clean their room they must! Why does this work? It is effective because of one simple fact: in order for the conscious mind to consider the choice you gave them, the unconscious mind must accept everything else as true, hence it is true that they will clean their room.

Sneaky Phrases: these are words or phrases in the English language that automatically trigger a human predisposition to react in a certain way. The great news is that the listener probably won't even be aware of the predisposition they have.

They are often everyday phrases or words that we use without realizing their power. Once you appreciate how to use them, however, they can transform your negotiations. Even better, the listener will have heard these phrases so often that they won't see the persuasion within them.

Examples include:

'Don't': I know, it sounds contradictory to tell someone not to do something, but what's the first thing that happens when you tell someone 'don't think about the money'. That's right, they automatically think about the money! That's the way the brain works. It first thinks about the money in order to not think about the money, but guess what? It's already thought about it!

'You can': 'You can shut the door'… here you are giving someone permission to do what you want them to do, and they'll do it! They won't know why, but their subconscious has accepted it as a command so they will obey.

Tag questions such as 'Isn't It', ' Can't you', 'Wouldn't you'? These are essentially negative questions tagged onto the end of a sentence, which people naturally want to answer straight away. 'You can see the genius in this, can't you?' Your listener will nod or shake his or her head instinctively, even if they don't quite know what they're agreeing to.

This is an effective negotiation that encourages a positive frame of mind. The trick is to add the tag question but treat it like a statement, so you don't raise your voice at the end. This confuses the conscious mind and instead the subconscious mind accepts it as fact.

<u>Embedded Commands:</u> finally, it's worth taking some time to practice adding straightforward embedded commands into your conversation. Your listener won't pick up on these consciously, but they will do the job nevertheless.

For example, *"I'm not here to tell you to trust me, but I know that you will want to be principled in your negotiation, and I can help with that. You can let down your guard and let me show you how to achieve your goal."*

The commands deeply embedded in this sentence include:
Trust me;
Be principled in your negotiation;
Let down your guard;
Let me show you;

The subconscious mind will pick up on these commands without the listener being aware of it;
Negotiation should be much easier as a result.

Research suggests the more presuppositions you use and the more you stack them on top of one another, the more you will distract the conscious, critical mind.

The conscious brain gives up trying to make sense of the sequence of events and stops analyzing. That's when the subconscious more accepting part of the brain takes over.

That's what you want. After all, it's the critical conscious brain that says 'no' or rejects agreements; get that out of the way, and you should enjoy significantly more negotiation success.

The Most Powerful Words in the English Language

Have you ever wondered which words hold the most weight in the English language? Which ones do we use the most, or which encourage us to perform in a particular way? We're keen to examine the latter, of course, because we'd like to use language to 'encourage people to yes' (to agree with us, to reach a settlement, to buy our product or give us a raise).

At first glance, these all-powerful words are pretty normal but, as we learned with our sneak phrases, they are hidden gems. They're so normal that no-one recognizes the inbuilt persuasion behind them and they hit their mark unconsciously.

So, what are these influential words? Drum roll please...

The most powerful words in the English language are...
And, Because...

Oh, what do you mean, you're a little disappointed? Are they not as all-singing and dancing as you expected? Well, give me the chance to show you them in action before you make up your mind.

Words such as 'because' and 'and' (and a few others as well) are linguistic bridges or linking words that allow us to create a stream of ideas without stopping in-between. They allow us to move from one idea to another to another, from one persuasive point to the next, without it being recognized by the conscious mind of our listener. Instead, they help to make associations in the subconscious and tend to be believed just by virtue of their use.

What reaction, for instance, do the following sentences inspire?
"I can't do that because my father died."
"I can't do it because it doesn't feel right."
"Why won't you do it? – Because I don't have time."

What do you think would happen if you said any of these to someone? I can tell you their reaction. Most people will simply accept what you say as long as you use the word because. As soon as we hear the word because, the brain associates it with a reason to not do (or do) something, and therefore automatically believes what came before it without question. 'I can't do that because…'

That's the beauty of language. We make sense of the communication around us by making associations between word. We assume that using the word, because, automatically backs up the statement made before it, even when or if it doesn't.

I recently tried it out (in a tongue-in-cheek fashion, it must be said) and it worked a treat. Friends asked me if I wanted to go out that night (and I just couldn't be bothered), so I said, "Sorry, I can't because I just don't want to."

Yes, you would have thought they'd smack me around the head for my cheek, wouldn't you? Instead, they snickered, shrugged and said, "Fair enough." And these are people who never usually let you off the hook! It worked!

Let's look briefly at the power of 'and', next.

And works in a similar way in that the brain associates it with cause and effect. Consider these classic hypnotist phrases:
"Close your eyes and picture a calming scene."
"Close your eyes and feel your body getting heavier."

Of course, you don't need to close your eyes for either of these things to happen, but the beauty of and is that it allows you to connect two pieces of unrelated information or experiences together and people will assume the first is causing the second. That could be very handy if you want to sway someone to believe in cause and effect during a negotiation.

"Let me show you and you'll understand what an opportunity this is."
"Buy this book and you'll never feel lost again."
The listener now assumes that if they do the first part, they will experience the second. Well done! You have persuaded them to make a sale or to give you the chance to demonstrate your opportunity.

I've only just touched the surface of persuasive language patterns here, but hopefully, you can see why they are so useful in negotiations. There are also dozens of other examples I could give you, but they won't all fit into this chapter. I would urge you to seek further research, books or training courses to learn more about the linguistic art of persuasion.

Something tells me you won't regret it.

<u>A Quick Word about Ethics</u>
You may wonder just how ethical it is to use subconscious persuasion on clients and fellow negotiators; aren't we manipulating them?

In a way, you could say that we are, but I think it's all a matter of intention. Hopefully, you've learned enough throughout the rest of this book to recognize that strong relationships are at the heart of effective negotiations. Treating your negotiating counterpart with respect is crucial if you want to avoid the usual adversarial skirmishes.

That said, there is nothing wrong with giving yourself a helping hand and using all the tools you have at your disposal.

Persuasive language isn't exclusive; anyone can learn it, therefore, it isn't an unfair advantage.
Neither can you make someone do something if they really don't want to.

True, done well, you can lower their defenses, quieten their critical mind and potentially get them to accept your premise subconsciously. However, you can't make someone do anything that is against their deeply ingrained moral code.

Persuasive language is just as viable a tool as body language and you probably wouldn't think twice about taking advantage of that. Ditto, the principles of persuasion.

After all, as persuasion guru, Robert Cialdini, said: *"Persuasion skills exert a far greater influence over others' behavior than formal power structures do."*

That gives us all a chance to be great negotiators, doesn't it? No matter where we stand in the hierarchy – at work, at home, between friends – we can change our world if we learn how to persuade effectively.

I hope this book sends you well on your way to success.

www.ingramcontent.com/pod-product-compliance
Lightning Source LLC
Chambersburg PA
CBHW031426210526
45464CB00005B/2073